VOICES OF MAN
The Meaning and Function of Language

MARIO PEI

AMS PRESS
NEW YORK

VOICES OF MAN
The Meaning and Function of Language

MARIO PEI

New York and Evanston
HARPER & ROW, PUBLISHERS

Library of Congress Cataloging in Publication Data

Pei, Mario Andrew, 1901-
    Voices of man.

    Reprint of the 1962 ed., which was issued as v. 29
of the World perspectives series.
    1. Language and languages. I. Title.
[P105.P44 1972]   400   71-173940
ISBN 0-404-07928-8

From the edition of 1962, New York
First AMS edition published in 1972
Manufactured in the United States of America

International Standard Book Number: 0-404-07928-8

AMS PRESS INC.
NEW YORK, N.Y.   10003

Contents

VOICES OF MAN

The Meaning and Function of Language

A Brief History of Linguistics

SPEECH is basically an automatic, unconscious process. It is therefore natural to assume that it must have been in use for thousands of years before any conscious thought about it arose.

Since our records of language necessarily cannot go back beyond the invention of writing and the first written documents, the only chronological link we can establish between language and the consciousness of language is to be sought in our earliest written records. The latter display an awareness of certain phases of language that indicates the possibility of an earlier linguistic consciousness, of which we cannot have direct proof.

The First Book of Genesis in the Bible, with its reference to the Tower of Babel and the confusion of tongues, shows that there was a realization of the diversity of tongues, coupled with clear appreciation of the all-important role that language plays in human coordinated activity, and even a longing for universal linguistic understanding.

In addition, bilingual glossaries, in Sumerian and Assyrian, are historically attested, while Egyptian hieroglyphic carvings show the arrival at the court of the Pharaohs of foreign ambassadors accompanied by interpreters.

Can all this be said to indicate the presence of a true linguistic consciousness in remote antiquity? Or merely awareness of language diversity and its inconveniences?[1]

At all events, it is not until the fourth century B.C. that we have, from ancient India and ancient Greece, records of an awareness of some, though by no means all, the problems posed by language. Panini's grammar of the Sanskrit language is a highly analytic, descriptive work, in which the sounds, system of accentuation and grammatical structure of India's ancient tongue are accurately and painstakingly presented. What is missing from the Indian picture is any attempt at comparison with other tongues, description of historical development, and philosophical or psychological interpretation. It may also be worth noting that at the time of the appearance of Panini's Sanskrit grammar the Sanskrit language had already flourished as a literary tongue for over fifteen hundred years, and that Panini himself makes reference to earlier grammatical works not available to us.

The Greeks, being primarily philosophers, were the first to enter into a full discussion of the nature of language, as distinguished from its physical, outward, observable features. In Plato's *Cratylus,* one of the disputants, Cratylus, favors the view that language is a natural phenomenon (*physis*), a gift that the gods have bestowed on man, and that the names of things are not mere symbols, but an inherent and essential part of the objects they stand for. Another participant, Hermogenes, holds that language is a matter of convention (*nomos, thesis*), and that a thing or action has a given name solely because men have agreed to accept the name as the symbol of the object in question. This idea of language as arbitrary convention today has general acceptance, and colors the thinking of most descriptive linguists. Aristotle later sponsored it by presenting language as a social contract. In the second century B.C., the grammarians Aristarchus and Crates held diverging views concerning language as a coherent system governed by laws (*analogy*), or as marked by irregularities ungoverned by laws (*anomaly*). Hence it may be said that two of the most controversial points of present-day linguistics had their inception with the Greeks.

But if the Greeks were the first to discuss the philosophy of language, they were much slower than the Indians in coming to a satisfactory classification of the parts of speech in their language. It was not until the Alexandrine period (second century B.C.) that Dionysius Thrax presented the grammatical categories and terminology in the form that prevails today, and considering the precise formal distinctions that appear among the parts of speech in Greek, this slowness is surprising, as is Plato's initial error of classifying the adjective with the verb rather than with the noun (this on the "logical" ground that the noun represents the subject, and anything else is the predicate). But by the time the Stoics and the Alexandrians had finished their tasks, the grammatical outline of the Greek language was substantially what it is today, and it was this concept of grammar and the grammatical categories that persisted through Roman antiquity, the Middle Ages, the Renaissance and the modern centuries, to be challenged only in very recent times.

Both Indian and Greek grammarians were completely uninterested in comparing their languages with the numerous other languages of their period. Significant is the fact that the Greeks labeled the speakers of all languages but Greek as *barbaroi,* or "babblers." The greatest concession made by the Greeks to the comparative principle was to establish a distinction among the chief literary dialects of Greece. At a much later period (fifth century A.D.) the lexicographer Hesychius cites many dialectal and foreign forms, but this at a time when many of the languages he mentions were already extinct.

The Romans, slavishly imitating the grammatical models set by the Greeks, displayed a similar mentality. They also allowed languages like Punic, Etruscan, Gaulish, Iberian to go unrecorded and uncompared. There was philosophical speculation of sorts, exemplified in Lucretius (first century B.C.), who attempted to explain language as arising from animal cries (the beginning of onomatopoetic theories), and in Varro (also first century B.C.), who claimed that language is basically utilitarian. Varro is also said to be responsible for the first erroneous attempt at language classification, by his implication that Latin is descended from, rather than a sister language of Greek.

Both Greece and Rome produced numerous grammars of the Greek and Latin languages, all of the prescriptive, normative type, describing the language as it should be rather than as it is (that the spoken tongue differed considerably from the prescriptions of the grammarians and the language of literature is abundantly proved by textual and epigraphic evidence). One of the earliest indications of a consciousness of diversity between the grammatical and the spoken tongue is the statement of the rhetorician Quintilian (first century A.D.) that "*aliud esse latine loqui, aliud grammatice*" ("It is one thing to speak Latin, something else to speak grammatically"). This reveals, if not a condonation of divergences from the standard, at least a consciousness of their existence.

From here, testimonies of awareness begin to abound. Livy makes reference to Etruscan as the cultural language of an earlier period (fourth century B.C.). Cicero speaks at length of "rustic and archaic" forms of Latin, and of the use of interpreters in Rome for visitors from such outlying provinces as Spain and Africa. Other writers inform us that Latin was spoken with local accents not only in these provinces, but in Italy itself. Perhaps our best illustration of the spoken Latin of the period appears in the Appendix to the grammar of Probus, a grammarian who lived in the third century A.D., which lists over three hundred words and forms commonly mispronounced or otherwise mishandled. To the present-day linguist, the value of Probus' contribution is that he gives both the "correct" and the "incorrect" forms (sometimes he reverses them), and the "incorrect" versions are often the direct and immediate forerunners of later Romance forms. To the philosopher and student of social phenomena, his contribution lies in his awareness, even though coupled with condemnation, of the divergences from the language standard.

In the matter of linguistic consciousness, Priscian, a grammarian of the sixth century A.D., offers a division of words into roots and endings which reminds one of the present-day morphemic theory, and goes far beyond an earlier attempt by Aristotle. But for what concerns language comparison, despite the awareness of the existence of foreign tongues, there seems to have been very little inclination to study or record them.

At the beginning of the fifth century A.D., St. Jerome, who was enough of a language scholar to realize that the language of the Galatians in Asia Minor was very close to that of the Gauls who inhabited Treviri, also makes the statement that *"ipsa latinitas et regionibus quotidie mutetur et tempore"* ("The Latin language itself is changing daily, both region by region and with the passing of time"). His contemporary, St. Augustine, irked perhaps by carping criticisms concerning his use of vulgarisms in addressing his congregations, stated that *"melius est reprehendant grammatici quam non intellegant populi"* ("It is better that the grammarians should chide than that the people should not understand").

Christianity and the barbarian invasions had the effect of imparting dignity to non-Classical languages. The newcomers had to be converted, and conversion called for a direct propaganda effort in the languages of those to be propagandized. Numerous Bible translations began to appear, along with language aids for pilgrims and travelers, some of which are forerunners of the modern tourist or military phrase book. There are also numerous glosses (interlinear and marginal translations into the current spoken tongue) of words and phrases from an older Latin that was beginning to be forgotten.[2]

At the same time, philosophical and speculative interest in language and its problems waned. There is very little in the way of linguistic thought during the early Middle Ages, save for constant and boresome restatements of the positions established by Plato and Aristotle centuries before. Greek had been practically forgotten in the West. (The expression *"Graecum est, non legitur,"* ancestor of the modern "It's Greek to me," came into vogue at this period.) Such comparison as there was lay between the Latin of the Vulgate and that of the grammarians. Utilitarian grammars of a few languages appeared. (Aelfric's Latin grammar in Anglo-Saxon, around the year 1000, is one of the earliest.) Still, it occurred to no one to make direct comparisons. The two principal Semitic languages in use, Hebrew and Arabic, were codified by their own grammarians between the seventh and tenth centuries, but these grammarians were steeped in Greek tradition, and followed the model of the Alexandrian school.

It was not until the thirteenth century that a new interest in philosophical speculation about the nature of language appeared. It began with the concept of a "universal grammar," valid for all tongues, though with minor variations. Roger Bacon expressed the concept in these words: *"Grammatica una et eadem est secundum substantiam in omnibus linguis, licet accidentaliter varietur"* ("Grammar is one and the same in all languages so far as substance is concerned, but it may vary in particular details").[3]

The Greeks and Romans, deliberately ignoring all languages but their own, had implied, without affirming it, the existence of such a universal grammar. The medieval grammarians, more keenly aware of language differences, tried to reconcile them with their great concept of universality. This idea of a universal grammar into which all tongues must fit was not finally rejected until the late nineteenth and early twentieth centuries, and then, curiously enough, only to be revived by one of the greatest proponents of structural diversity, Benjamin Lee Whorf.[4]

Dante's *De Vulgari Eloquentia* of 1305 marked, in some ways, the beginning of modern linguistic thought. Dante made a true attempt at language derivation and language comparison, correctly describing Italian and its sister Romance languages as stemming from Latin. He offered a basically correct enumeration and classification of the Italian dialects, thus getting linguistic geography off to an early start. His description of the ideal Italian literary tongue as a conglomeration of dialects rather than a simple outgrowth of his own Florentine Tuscan is still open to controversy, and he oversimplifies when he defines the Italian *Volgare* as Latin without the rules of grammar. Yet he was the first to claim dignity for the new vernaculars, as against the crystallized Latin of universal medieval scholarship.

Dante's pronouncement was followed, at some distance of time, by the fall of Constantinople, with the consequent rediscovery of Greek by the West, as well as by voyages of exploration to Africa and Asia, and the discovery of the New World, with its myriad strange tongues. The fifteenth and sixteenth centuries were an era of language discovery and language study, marked by the appearance of numerous grammars of common western European vernaculars and Near Eastern tongues, then of such far-flung languages as the Nahuatl of Mexico and the Quichua of Peru. Dante's pronouncements concerning the vernacular of Italy set off a chain reaction of discussion and speculation, both in Italy and elsewhere. This led to the writing of numerous works concerning the proper use of the vernaculars, and even to the founding of the first language academy (the Accademia della Crusca, established in 1578). The question of language origins came up, and Juan de Valdés' *Diálogo de la lengua* of 1533 started a fashion in various countries. The problem of affiliation and classification of languages began to be discussed, by Scaliger and others.[5] Even dialectal divisions and the objective reality of esthetically unattractive language forms came in for an inning in H. Etienne's *Thesaurus linguae graecae* of 1572.

The theory of objectivity and the search for truth rather than fancy were furthered in the following century by Mabillon and Du Cange,[6] who established the rules for determining the authenticity and approximate dating of ancient texts. At the same time, there were further attempts at etymology (Ménage, *Origines de la langue française,* 1650, where about 72 per cent of the derivations are correct). There was further exploration of unusual languages, with grammars of Tagalog, Malay, Tamil, Georgian, Amharic, and numerous American Indian tongues. There were additional attempts at language classification, such as the one of Leibniz,[7] and there was an earnest continuation of the effort to reduce all grammars to a single universal grammar, as exemplified by the Port Royal Grammar of 1660.

The seventeenth and eighteenth centuries displayed much interest in languages and linguistics, but lacked a workable, working methodology. In the eighteenth century, there was great interest in the problem of the origin of language, coupled with some unsuccessful attempts at a comparative method, and the exploration of more unusual languages. The major contributions appeared in the field of Romance Philology, with Lacurne de Ste.-Palaye's insistence on the comparison of the Romance tongues,[8] Bonamy's stress on the *lingua rustica* of Gregory of Tours and of the Formulas of Angers as the true direct ancestors of the Romance vernaculars,[9] the monumental collections of medieval texts of

Flórez and Muratori,[10] and Martín Sarmiento's suggestion that a linguistic atlas of Galicia be undertaken.

At the close of the eighteenth century Sir William Jones presented his study on the intimate relationship of Sanskrit and Old Persian with Latin, Greek, Celtic and Germanic.[11] It is possible that the importance of Jones' "discovery" of Sanskrit has been overstressed; as far back as the sixteenth century, an Italian traveler, Sassetti, had drawn attention to the curious resemblances between Sanskrit and Italian; but such earlier observations had fallen on unfertile ground, like "discoveries" of America prior to Columbus. Jones' pronouncement, on the contrary, found a ripe field, and was quickly followed by a series of comparative studies which extended through the nineteenth century and comprised some of the most revered names in the field of linguistics.

The new methodology consisted in laying side by side forms taken from the oldest Indo-European languages, and from their comparison deriving the "laws" of their separate development, along with the reconstruction of the hypothetical Indo-European parent language from which they sprang.

F. von Schlegel[12] pointed the way in 1808 with the assertion that a comparative study of the grammar of Sanskrit and other languages would yield the same sort of information on the genealogy of language that comparative anatomy had made possible in natural history. Next came R. C. Rask's detailed study of Old Norse,[13] which offered in addition a regular system of phonological correspondences, a complete classification of the Indo-European languages, and even a statement of the Germanic consonant shift later elaborated by J. Grimm. Two years later, F. Bopp[14] did for comparative morphology what Rask had done for comparative phonology. Grimm[15] and Verner[16] round out the constellation of great names in the comparative field; but this work, which was to continue throughout the nineteenth century,

drew to its ranks many other illustrious researchers: F. Diez and
W. Meyer-Lübke, who codified the comparative approach for the
Romance branch of Indo-European; F. Miklosich and J. K.
Zeuss, who did the same thing, respectively, for Slavic and Celtic;
A. F. Pott, who drew up the definitive tables of Indo-European
phonological correspondences; Brugmann and Delbrück, who
gave the final touch to the comparative approach.[17]

The nineteenth-century spotlight was trained largely on the
dead languages and their historical development, but there were
two men who directed attention to the living languages and their
possibilities. One was Schleicher,[18] who offered living Lithuanian
as a language that by reason of its archaic, unchanged structure
presents reconstructive possibilities to an even greater degree than
Sanskrit, and suggested that the true basis for study should be not
so much the dead, static early tongues, but the living languages,
which are subject to change and fluctuation, and in which the
linguistic processes may be much better observed and made the
basis for our conclusions. The other was von Humboldt,[19] whose
research in non-Indo-European languages began to present a new
entrancing field of classification. Humboldt also formulated the
theory that language is the outer manifestation of a people's soul,
and the creator of their pattern of thought (a theory later picked
up and restated by Whorf). The human mind, Humboldt
claimed, is an active participant in the creation and development
of speech sounds, and language is a dynamic, not a static, phenomenon.

The second half of the century was marked by the outburst of
an angry controversy, when the Neo-Grammarian school,[20]
headed by such renowned figures as Brugmann, Osthoff, Paul and
Leskien, propounded the theory that language change operates
in accordance with phonological "laws" that have the same
stringency as the laws of the physical world; that in a given area

and at a given period a sound change, once initiated, will operate without exception. Opposition to this iron cogency of the *Lautgesetz* was voiced first by the Neo-Linguist school headed by Schuchardt, Bertoni, Curtius, Vossler, Ascoli and Bartoli,[21] then by a philosopher, Croce.[22] The Neo-Linguists held that sound changes are sporadic and individualistic phenomena, conditioned by the factor of dialects, which in the final analysis are as numerous as the speakers, and by linguistic substrata and superstrata. Languages, they held, do not exist in a vacuum; innovations are created by individuals, and then extended to the group. Croce not only held that language cannot be subject to any rigid laws of change; he offered instead the proposition that language is sound for the purpose of expression rather than of communication, that it is the individual, in his creative urge, who is the arbiter of change and innovation, and that just as the individual cannot be regimented, neither can language.

In reply to the cogent attacks of the Neo-Linguists, the Neo-Grammarians modified their position to the extent of admitting that their iron sound laws, while admitting of no exception, may nevertheless be conditioned by numerous extraneous factors, such as analogy and dialectal or learned borrowing. This admission meant that the two positions ceased to be irreconcilable, since now all apparent exceptions to the sound laws could be attributed to such factors. To borrow a simile from the world of physics, it is true that metal will expand uniformly with the application of higher temperatures, but only providing all other factors, such as pressure, are constant; a change in pressure as well as in temperature will be reflected in an apparent deviation from the invariable law of expansion.

The great controversy of the nineteenth century, however unfortunate it may have been by reason of the bitterness it engendered, nevertheless had its merits in stressing the need for precision in the study of language phenomena and in focusing attention on the problem of dialects and their infinite variety, and it may be said to have indirectly fostered linguistic geography and the linguistic atlases.

While the nineteenth century was dominated largely by the comparative, historical, diachronic approach to linguistics, the twentieth century, particularly since 1920, has been dominated by the general, descriptive, synchronic approach. This is best illustrated by De Saussure's definition of one of the purposes of general linguistics as "to seek out the forces operating permanently and universally in all languages" and "drawing up general laws from particular phenomena," which is faintly reminiscent of the universal grammar of the medieval scholars. Problems of language in general, as distinguished from the study of individual languages and their evolution, have come to the fore. Along with precise, physical-science laboratory techniques, we have philosophical discussions on the nature of language that remind us of the ancient Greeks.

The tone for the twentieth century was set by F. de Saussure's *Cours de linguistique générale* of 1916,[23] published after his death and compiled from notes taken by his students. In De Saussure's concept, language is basically a sociological phenomenon, and must be viewed in relation to its speakers and their psychological processes. This does not differ too widely from von Humboldt's concept, but De Saussure goes much farther. He insists upon a careful distinction between language, which is a system in which many individuals participate, and speech, the basic production of sounds peculiar to the individual speaker. The linguistic sign, in De Saussure's concept, is both arbitrary and constant, and a static, synchronic, descriptive element is essential to the speaker, while language change is largely a matter of convenience of articulation. The difference between language and dialect, and

the question of language classification, which had loomed so large
in the earlier century, are now in the background.

De Saussure's students and followers, among them Meillet,
Vendryes, Bally and Sommerfelt, continued to pursue detailed
historical and comparative studies, but in spite of this, the pre-
dominant slant of the past four decades has leaned heavily in
the direction of the descriptive as against the historical; of phonology and, to a lesser degree, morphology and syntax as against
etymology and semantics; of the spoken vernaculars as against the
written, literary languages; of the mechanical as against the
spiritual manifestations of language.

Linguistic geography, a fairly young branch of linguistics,
though heralded centuries earlier by Sarmiento, came to fruition
in the various linguistic atlases which give an over-all picture of
dialectal distribution based on precise field work rather than
generalizations.[24]

Several important developments in the most recent decades
have been due, directly or indirectly, to De Saussure's teachings.
There are Jespersen's theories[25] about progress in language rather
than decay due to historical evolution, coupled with implications
in the field of constructed languages for international use. There
is the phonemic theory, which interprets language function-
ally in terms of the language's sound pattern, and goes on to
a series of systematic sound oppositions, leading ultimately to the
structuralism of the Prague school and its followers. (Language
appears and develops as a unit, not as a series of individual and
unrelated changes.)[26] There is the American or anthropological
extension of this school of thought, which begins with the works
of Boas, Sapir, Bloomfield,[27] and continues with Harris, Fries,
Hockett[28] and numerous others. The thinking of the American
school is colored by strong leanings in favor of a purely descriptive
approach, with stress on phonology and the spoken tongue, and a

corresponding irreverence for everything historical and traditional, including the written language and past achievements in
the linguistic field.

Other recent developments are the Marxian school of linguistics, dominated by the teachings of Marr, who stressed language
as a social class phenomenon (but Marr's ideas were disavowed
by Stalin) ;[29] the "Linguistic Alliance" theory of the Prague school
(languages in geographical and historical contact influence one
another and tend to evolve along parallel lines) ;[30] the attempts of
Brøndal and Hjelmslev to achieve a new classification of the parts
of speech and grammatical categories (Glossematics) ;[31] the much
discussed theory of Metalinguistics brought into vogue by Whorf
(the type of language habitually spoken colors the thinking and
behavior of the speakers).[32]

A by-product of the work of the American school is the doctrine of permissiveness or "usage" in language. ("Language is
what people speak, not what someone thinks they ought to
speak.")[33] Taken at its maximum, this doctrine sanctifies usage
and makes it paramount over prescriptive grammar, giving full
currency and encouragement to all innovations, slang and
dialectal forms, and making them equal in practical value with the
standard language, while at the same time it discredits the written
form of the language as an archaic survival and reveres the
spoken tongue as the only "true" language. A secondary feature
of the Americanistic doctrine is the tendency to regard all languages as of equal importance, regardless of their size, extent, or
the contributions their speakers may have made to the world's
civilization.[34]

Along with these controversial and partly philosophical aspects
of present-day linguistics, attention may be called to outstanding
achievements in the purely objective field of physiological phonetics, as illustrated by the work of Sievers, Rousselot, Fouché,

Grammont and Pike, among others;[35] in the detailed study of ancient languages (Sturtevant, Buck, Conway, Whatmough are among the best-known names in this field) ;[36] in linguistic geography (Gilliéron and Edmont, Jud and Jaberg, Kurath, Pop) ;[37] in the reconstruction of the Indo-European parent language (Kurilowicz, Pokorny) ;[38] and in the field of possible broader relationships between Indo-European and other language families (Trombetti, Cuny, Collinder).[39]

*   *   *   *

Such, along brief, vastly oversimplified lines, is the history of what men have thought about language, and the treatment they have given the subject.

This treatment leaves us with a number of unsolved problems, many of which, by their very nature, may never be solved, but only discussed and rediscussed. This has actually taken place numerous times throughout history, though participants have changed, battlegrounds have shifted, and the very names of movements and schools have been disguised so that their basic identity has become unrecognizable.

It is not, and cannot be, our purpose to offer an ultimate solution for these problems. We can only present a further discussion and a very small number of novel considerations, while at the same time synthesizing the problems and bringing them up to date.

NOTES TO "A BRIEF HISTORY OF LINGUISTICS"

1. For the historical discussion that follows, see: R. E. Robins, *Ancient and Medieval Grammatical Theory in Europe,* London, 1951, pp. 7, 19–57, 64; L. H. Gray, *Foundations of Language,* New York, 1937, pp. 419–460; A. Monteverdi, *Manuale di avviamento agli studi romanzi,* Milano, 1952, pp. 4, 36, 40–44, 47. For a more extended discussion of the history of linguistic thought, see: H. Steinthal, *Geschichte der Sprachwissenschaft bei den Griechen und Römern,* Berlin, 1863; T.

Benfey, *Geschichte der Sprachwissenschaft,* München, 1869; G. Devoto, *I Fondamenti della storia linguistica,* Firenze, 1951; H. Pedersen, *Linguistic Science in the 19th Century* (tr. J. Spargo), Cambridge, 1931.

2. W. Foerster and E. Koschwitz, *Altfranzösisches Uebungsbuch,* Heilbronn, 1884, pp. 1–43.

3. Robins, *op. cit.,* p. 77.

4. See chapters "Grammatical Categories," and "Language: Plan and Conception of Arrangement," in *Language, Thought and Reality* (ed. J. B. Carroll), Cambridge, 1956.

5. J. J. Scaliger, *Diatriba de Europaeorum Linguis,* 1599.

6. J. Mabillon, *De Re Diplomatica,* 1681; D. D. du Cange, *Glossarium ad Scriptores Mediae et Infimae Latinitatis,* 1678.

7. G. W. von Leibniz, *Brevis Designatio Meditationum de Originibus Gentium,* 1710.

8. Lacurne de Ste.-Palaye, *Dictionnaire historique de l'ancien français,* Niort, 1875–82.

9. P. N. Bonamy, *Réflexions sur la langue latine vulgaire,* Hague, 1751.

10. E. Flórez, *España sagrada,* Madrid, 1749 (new Real Academia ed., 1952); L. A. Muratori, *Antiquitates Italicae Medii Aevi,* Arezzo, 1773–1780.

11. Sir Wm. Jones, "Third Annual Discourse on the Hindus" (Feb. 2, 1786), in *Works of Sir William Jones* (coll. by L. Teignmouth), London, 1807.

12. F. von Schlegel, *Ueber die Sprache und Weisheit der Indier,* 1808.

13. R. C. Rask, *Investigation of the Origin of Old Norse or Icelandic,* 1814.

14. F. Bopp, *Ueber das Conjugationssystem der Sanskritsprache,* 1816.

15. J. Grimm, *Deutsche Grammatik,* 1819–1840; *Geschichte der deutschen Sprache,* 1848–1867.

16. K. Verner, "Eine Ausnahme der ersten Lautverschiebung," *Zeitschrift für vergleichende Sprachforschung,* XXIII (1877), pp. 97–130.

17. F. Diez, *Grammatik der romanischen Sprachen,* 1836–1844; W. Meyer-Lübke, *Grammatik der romanischen Sprachen,* 1890–1902; F. Miklosich, *Vergleichende Grammatik der slavischen Sprachen,* 1874–1879; J. K. Zeuss, *Grammatica Celtica,* 1853; K. Brugmann and K. Delbrück, *Grundriss der vergleichenden Grammatik der indogermanischen Sprachen,* 1886–1900.

18. A. Schleicher, *Compendium of Comparative Grammar of the Indo-European Languages,* 1861.

19. W. von Humboldt, *Ueber die Kawisprache,* 1836–1837.

20. I. Iordan and J. Orr, *Introduction to Romance Philology,* London,

1937, pp. 15–19. See also H. Paul, *Prinzipien der Sprachgeschichte*, 1880, for a summation of the Neogrammarian position.

21. Iordan and Orr, *op. cit.*, pp. 86–143. See also M. Bartoli, *Introduzione alla Neolinguistica*, 1925, for a summation of the Neolinguist position.

22. B. Croce, *Estetica come scienza*, Bari, 1912; *Filosofia del linguaggio*, Bari, 1924.

23. English translation by W. Baskin, *Course in General Linguistics*, New York, 1959.

24. J. Gilliéron and E. Edmont, *Atlas linguistique de la France*, 1902–1910; K. Jaberg and J. Jud, *Sprach- und Sachatlas Italiens und der Südschweiz*, 1928–1940; H. Kurath, *Linguistic Atlas of New England*, 1939–1943; etc.

25. O. Jespersen, *Language, its Nature, Development and Origin*, 1922; *The Philosophy of Grammar*, 1924.

26. N. Trubetskoy, *Grundzüge der Phonologie*, 1939; R. Jakobson, *Kindersprache, Aphasie, und allgemeine Lautgesetze*, 1942; A. Martinet, *Economie des changements phonétiques*, 1955.

27. F. Boas, *Handbook of American Indian Languages*, 1907–1911; E. Sapir, *Language*, 1921; L. Bloomfield, *Language*, 1933.

28. Z. Harris, *Methods in Structural Linguistics*, 1951; C. Fries, *The Structure of English*, 1952; C. Hockett, *Course in Modern Linguistics*, 1958; B. Bloch and G. Trager, *Outline of Linguistic Analysis*, 1942; J. B. Carroll, *The Study of Language*, 1953; H. A. Gleason, *Introduction to Descriptive Linguistics*, 1955; N. Brooks, *Language and Language Learning*, 1960; etc. For a reasoned criticism of this school of thought, see J. Whatmough, *Language; a Modern Synthesis*, 1956.

29. J. V. Murra, R. M. Hankin and F. Holling, *The Soviet Linguistic Controversy*, 1951.

30. U. Weinreich, *Languages in Contact*, 1953.

31. V. Brøndal, *Les Parties du discours*, Copenhagen, 1928; *Essais de linguistique générale*, Copenhagen, 1943; L. Hjelmslev, *Catégorie des cas*, Aarhus, 1935–1937; *Prolegomena to a Theory of Language* (tr. F. Whitefield), Baltimore, 1953; *Recherches structurales*, Copenhagen, 1949; L. Hjelmslev and H. J. Uldall, *Outline of Glossematics*, Copenhagen, 1957.

32. See note 4.

33. Bloch and Trager, *op. cit.*, p. 9; L. Bloomfield, *Outline Guide for the Practical Study of Foreign Languages*, 1942, p. 16.

34. This view is generally implied rather than expressly stated; see L. Bloomfield, "Philosophical Aspects of Language," *Studies in the History of Culture*, 1942, pp. 178–184.

35. E. Sievers, *Grundzüge der Phonetik*, 1901; P. J. Rousselot, *Prin-*

cipes de phonétique expérimentale, 1897–1909; P. Fouché, *Etudes de phonétique générale,* 1927; M. Grammont, *Traité de phonétique,* 1933; K. L. Pike, *Phonetics,* 1943.

36. E. H. Sturtevant, *Comparative Grammar of the Hittite Language,* 1933; *Pronunciation of Greek and Latin,* 1940; C. D. Buck, *A Grammar of Oscan and Umbrian,* 1928; R. G. Kent, *The Sounds of Latin,* 1932; R. S. Conway, J. Whatmough, and S. E. Johnston, *The Prae-Italic Dialects of Italy,* 1933.

37. See note 24. See also H. Kurath, *A Word Geography of the Eastern United States,* 1948; S. Pop, *La Dialectologie,* 1950.

38. J. Kurilowicz, *Etudes indo-européennes,* 1935; J. Pokorny, *Indogermanisches etymologisches Wörterbuch,* 1951–1962.

39. A. Trombetti, *L'unità d'origine del linguaggio,* 1905; *Elementi di glottologia,* 1922–1923; A. Cuny, *Etudes prégrammaticales sur le domaine des langues indo-européennes et chamito-sémitiques,* 1924; B. Collinder, *Indo-uralisches Sprachgut,* 1934.

The Origin and Nature of Language

THESE are twin problems, linked, yet separate. For what concerns language's origin, we have legend, tradition, philosophical discussion, but no scientific facts.

Many races and groups view language as a gift conferred upon man by God, or the gods. In those traditions where this is not specifically stated (as in our own Bible), it is at least implied.

The discussion in Plato's *Cratylus* as to whether language arises from *physis* or from *nomos* is perhaps the first indication of skepticism in this regard. "Nature" may be accepted as a substitute for God. But the specific problem of origin is by-passed by Hermogenes as he presents his "conventional" thesis. If men agree to use certain sequences of sounds to symbolize certain objects, the sound sequences must yet have their inception somewhere.

Most modern quasi-scientific theories as to the origin of language are based on one or another variant of the onomatopoeic process. One, the *ding-dong* theory, comes dangerously close to the *physis* idea of the ancients, as it depends upon some sort of mystic link between sound and sense. The others are far more materialistic. The *bow-wow* theory, which has perhaps the greatest vogue, holds that language rose in imitation of sounds heard in nature, as when a child says *baa-baa* to designate a sheep after hearing its bleating, or *choo-choo* to describe a train with its assorted noises. There is no question that this theory accounts for the creation of words described in the dictionaries as echoic (*crash, clang, buzz,* etc.), but whether the echoic process can be extended to account for the origin of all words is doubtful. There is a further obstacle to its acceptance in the known fact that speakers of different languages seem to hear natural sounds in different ways, and imitate them in such a fashion that altogether different words come into being. English hears as *bow-wow* or *woof-woof* what French hears as *oua-oua,* and Italian as *bu-bu;* the cock's crowing is variously *cock-a-doodle-doo, chicchirichì, cocorico;* only the cat's *meow* seems to be international.

An extension of the *bow-wow* theory is the *pooh-pooh,* which holds that words began to be formed out of original ejaculations of pleasure, fear, surprise, etc., such as are produced by apes; this would make the interjection the original language unit and part of speech. The *sing-song* theory presents the vocalization of primitive rhythmic chants as the source of words that ultimately turn into language. A kinesthetic origin is favored by the *yo-he-ho* theory (language arises as a series of reflex grunts accompanying physical exertion, like the *ey ukhnem* of the Volga boatmen); and by the *ta-ta* theory (language arises as the vocal organs try to imitate movements performed by other parts of the body).

It goes without saying that all these theories are unproved and unprovable. There may be, and undoubtedly is, an element of truth in all of them, as each one appears to have some application in language creations that go on under our own eyes. Whether they can be applied, individually or as a group, to the entire language process, is something else.

Against them stands one imposing fact. If they were true, language would have arisen as a series of isolated, monosyllabic grunts, groans and wheezes, later refined and combined to form words. We might then expect to find such a language in use among primitive and backward groups with a low standard of civilization. Such is emphatically not the case. The opposite is rather true. The tongues of primitive groups are, as a rule, complex in structure, while the languages of the more civilized groups appear to be more complex and involved the farther we go back into their history, and tend to simplify as we approach their modern stage. Of course, there is nothing to prevent us from saying that all languages evolved from the grunt-and-groan stage to the various forms in which they appear historically, and that some of them, like Chinese and English, then went through a historically attested process of simplification and reduction to a more analytic, monosyllabic structure. This is, however, somewhat hard to believe when we come to the structurally complex languages of groups that in other respects still live in the Stone Age.

One more quasi-scientific theory is worth mentioning. It is to the effect that as the human being assumed an erect posture, the contour of his brain was altered so that the evolution of the speech centers became possible. Here again, evidence is largely lacking. Other primates beside man normally walk upright, but without such evolution.

It is only natural that in their desire to cast light upon the origin of language, experimenters should have studied the growth of the speech process in the human child. Carried on with normal children in normal environments, such studies are thoroughly inconclusive from the standpoint of the origin of language. All they indicate is a process of imitation of the older members of the social group.

There are at least three historical instances of potentates who tried the experiment of isolating children from birth to see if they would develop some form of language not based on imitation of their elders. Herodotus tells us of the Egyptian Pharaoh Psam-

metichus, who tried the experiment on two children, and from
the fact that their first spoken word sounded like *bekos,* Phrygian
for "bread," decided that Phrygian must have been the original
language. Frederick II, at the beginning of the thirteenth century,
tried a similar experiment, but the children are reported to have
died before any definite result could be obtained. James IV of
Scotland, around 1500, was the third experimenter, and he reported that his guinea pigs came out speaking fair Hebrew.
Scientific controls having been lacking in all three experiments, no
conclusion can be drawn from them, particularly for what concerns the origin of language.

This part of the problem, it seems, is insoluble. If language
arose as "convention," how was the convention arrived at, save in
terms of pre-existing language? If it arose by "nature," what do
we mean by "nature"? Blind chance? An intelligent Supreme
Being? If any of the onomatopoeic theories are true, why are they
not illustrated in any language of which we have a record?

It is small wonder that linguists, as apart from philosophers,
have renounced the topic of language's origin, to the point where
the Société de Linguistique of Paris banned this subject as a
topic for papers. It continues, however, to fascinate the minds of
those who are speculatively rather than scientifically inclined. As
samples of recent thought on the subject, the reader is referred to
O. Jespersen, *Language, its Nature, Development and Origin,*
1922; R. Paget, *Human Speech,* 1930; G. Revesz, *Ursprung und
Vorgeschichte der Sprache,* Bern, 1946 (or, in translation,
Origins and Prehistory of Language, New York, 1956); R. A.
Wilson, *The Miraculous Birth of Language,* New York, 1949;
A. S. Diamond, *The History and Origin of Language,* New York,
1959; and N. J. Jacobs' somewhat whimsical *Naming Day in
Eden,* New York, 1948.[1]

When we move on to the nature of language, we stand on more

solid ground. To the question "Is language a natural or a conventional phenomenon?", not in its origin, but in its functioning, the answer first given by Hermogenes and Aristotle (language is a matter of convention, or, better yet, a social contract) is expanded and clarified in very recent times by the definition given by De Saussure: "the linguistic sign is both arbitrary and constant." "Arbitrary" means that there is no inherent link between the thing signified and the word that signifies it; "constant" means that in a given speech community the same sign (or word, or expression) must be used by all the speakers (with, perhaps, permissible variations which do not distort it beyond comprehension), and in the same meaning (with the same permissive range). If these conditions are not met, language ceases to be meaningful, which is tantamount to saying that it ceases to be language.

The link is not between the word and the object; it is between the word and the concept of the object which exists in the speaker's mind. At the same time, another link must exist among the various and varied minds of the members of the speech community.

Two things stand out from De Saussure's definition. One is the indissoluble connection between language and meaning, or, to put it another way, between language and the mind (both the personal mind of the individual speaker, and the collective mind of the community). This mental aspect of language is all too often forgotten or minimized by the very linguists who pay the highest lip service to De Saussure, as will be seen.

The second item, more relevant to the present discussion, is the definition of the linguistic sign as arbitrary. A moment's reflection will suffice to convince us of the truth of this proposition. If the linguistic sign were not as De Saussure describes it, if there were a real link between the word and the object, all people would be using the same language. Each object would be accompanied by its own intrinsic sign.

Even if it were to be claimed that in origin such intrinsic signs existed, and that they changed as languages diverged, the proposition would still stand that as of today the signs are different. Naive monoglot speakers of each language think their sign is intrinsically bound to the object it denotes, like the old lady who wondered why foreigners had to have such strange words as *Brot, pain* and *hlyeb* for what was so obviously "bread." But it is as natural for the Russian speaker to link *hlyeb* with his mental picture of a loaf of bread as it was for the old American lady to couple the mental image of a loaf with the spoken English word *bread.*

Leaving the question of language origin out of consideration, it is undeniable that at the present moment, and as far back in history as the records will allow us to go, language is a matter of convention, and that *nomos* and *thesis* easily carry the day against *physis.*

There is a rather obvious parallel between language and the various forms of currency in use today. Money, all economists agree, is only a symbol of purchasing power, of the ability to enter into possession of the thing one really desires to possess. Save where the transaction takes the actual form of barter (in which case one can no longer speak of money), the intrinsic value of the form of currency is unimportant, and often negligible. Checks and paper currency are intrinsically worth only the paper on which they are inscribed. Even gold and silver have only limited value for purposes of adornment, and for more practical purposes are worth less than hardier metals. The only real value of currency is what the community decides it shall have. If the community's decision changes, as in periods of inflation or shortage of real commodities, the symbol of purchasing power quickly changes its value, even to the point of losing it altogether.

In like manner, the linguistic symbol is of value only insofar as the community decides to accept it. If the community changes its mind, the language symbol changes or loses its value. If you move from one to another speech community, your language is worthless, just as your paper currency is worthless, unless you get it changed. In the case of language, the change takes the form of a translation.

There is one additional factor in our simile between language and money that is often lost sight of or minimized. In the case of currency, you may have either direct or indirect symbolization. Gold and silver coin may be described as direct symbols of purchasing power. Paper currency is a promise to pay in gold or silver, which makes it a symbol of a symbol. A check, draft or money order is a promise to pay in paper, which is in turn a promise to pay in metal, which is in turn a symbol of purchasing power. Hence we have not only a symbol, but also a symbol of a symbol of a symbol. It is all very well to speak of gold and silver coin as being the originator of all other forms of monetary symbolization, and having historical priority; that makes it no less convenient for me, in the twentieth century and in a civilized country, to prefer receiving a payment due me in the form of paper currency, or, better yet, of a check.

Writing, and other symbolic forms of language that do not involve the speech organs, are likewise symbols of the spoken tongue. In western alphabetic forms, they are imperfect attempts to symbolize the sounds of the spoken tongue. In other writing systems, notably the Chinese, they symbolize objects and concepts, but still they symbolize such objects and concepts in the form and order they would assume in speech.

Again, we can grant historical priority to speech as a symbol of concepts common to an entire speech community. But again we may find it more convenient and satisfactory to "take our payment" (give and receive our ideas) in written or other indirect symbolic form.

Both from a practical and from a philosophical standpoint, the paramount importance which some schools of linguistics bestow upon the spoken form of language is largely unwarranted. From the standpoint of historical priority, there is the possibility (though not the probability) that some form of pictorial representation may have antedated speech. From the standpoint of universality, gestural language and the "language" of facial expressions and bodily movements are just as widespread as speech. That our primary system of communication of thoughts is speech rather than gesture is probably due to the fact that speech can operate in the dark and around obstacles that obstruct the view, and that it leaves the hands free for other simultaneous operations.

All this, at any rate, pertains to the seemingly insoluble problem of the origin of language. For what concerns the nature of language as it has operated within the memory of man, there is no denying its conventional, symbolical, arbitrary and constant features, its link with the minds of the speakers, its fundamental purpose, which is the transfer of meaning from one human mind to another.

NOTE TO PROBLEM I

1. It is of interest to compare these recent works with an older one, such as J. G. von Herder, *Abhandlung über den Ursprung der Sprache,* 1772.

Logic and Universality in Language

THE problem of logic in language has links both with the origin and nature of language and with the question of linguistics and semantics.

Is language logical? Ought it to be logical? If language originates as a gift from above, then it is logical to suppose that this gift would conform to the logical scheme prescribed by a higher intelligence. If it originates as a matter of convention, then chance is uppermost, and it is vain to look for logic in what is arbitrary. If there is an intrinsic relationship between the word and the object, then there is a corresponding underlying relationship between the form and the meaning. But if the connection between signifier and signified is purely arbitrary, then form and meaning are independent of each other.

The ancients did not specifically state their belief in a universal grammar applicable to all languages, mainly because all languages did not interest them. Restricting their study, as did the Indians, to Sanskrit alone, or, as did the Greeks, to Greek alone, or even, as did the Romans, to Greek and Latin, the grammatical outline that resulted in each case was bound to be not merely that of the language under consideration, but, by implication, that of all language worthy of the name.

While the Indians achieved a satisfactory classification of the grammatical concepts and the parts of speech at an early date, it took the Greeks a surprisingly long time to attain the same results. The Indians focused their attention upon the forms of their language and the functions served by those forms. The Greeks were preoccupied with making their language fit into a logical mold, and their observation of form and function, as against meaning and function, came late.

Yet when the Greeks finally achieved a full statement of grammatical categories and parts of speech, their classification was well-nigh perfect, and stood the test of time. This classification was achieved by what a modern linguist could only describe as a mixture of methods. On the one hand we have such formal distinctions as the early discovery by Protagoras that there was agreement by gender, and Aristotle's later classification of genders by the test of endings. On the other hand, the same Aristotle based his distinctions on meaning when he described the word as the smallest meaningful unit, and applied his definition to the resolution of compound nouns into their constituent elements, thus antedating Bloomfield's minimum free form, or morpheme.[1] The Stoics not only distinguished between form and meaning, they also invented the Saussurian signifier and signified, created the first school of phonetics, and even devised the nonsense words which are so current today in the illustrations of linguistic scientists who refuse to let meaning enter their analysis.[2]

Yet it remained for the Middle Ages to formulate in specific terms the theory of a universal grammar, applicable to all languages, on the basis of the grammatical categories and parts of speech finally achieved by Dionysius Thrax and the Alexandrine School.[3] While others of the medieval Modistae may have expressed the principle at greater length, we can find no more concise and comprehensive a statement than that of Roger Bacon, to the effect that "in substance, grammar is one and the same in all languages, but it may vary accidentally."[4]

One grammar for the world! But if such a grammar exists, it must of necessity be logical, since it is universal, and any divergence from it is an idiosyncrasy, an aberration.

This is precisely the way in which the grammatical-logical problem was viewed and treated, down to the end of the nineteenth century, despite the ever-growing accumulation of linguistic evidence to the contrary. This point of view is evident even in the first attempts at a constructed language, as formulated by Descartes and his contemporaries: a language so simple that it can be learned without effort by anyone, by reason of its absolute regularity *and absolute logic,* and a word-coining system whereby there will be, among the ideas of the human mind, the same order that prevails among numbers in mathematics, so that just as in mathematics there is a logical progression from the known to the unknown, the same may be possible with words.[5]

To what extent this preoccupation with logic hampered the study of both language and languages may be left to the imagination. Language is logical enough in its purpose, which is the transfer of meaning; but not in its procedure, which varies enormously from tongue to tongue.

Yet, if language fails utterly to have the same structure throughout, it has its own intrinsic, logical, universal qualities, which can be reduced to some sort of universal, logical scheme. All languages, without exception, have to have a set of phonemes, or sounds which are distinctively significant to the speakers; a set of words, which betoken objects, actions and concepts; a set of grammatical forms, which may be chiefly morphological (that is, consisting of endings, prefixes, or changes within the word to convey modifications of basic meanings), or chiefly syntactical (that is, based on the order in which the words are uttered).

Beyond that, it may be safely asserted that all languages are all-pervasive within their respective communities; that they are all normally a reflex, instinctive action once they are properly acquired; that they are all geographically localized, socially stratified, subject to change, but also to standardizing influences; and that they are, in their respective sound-and-form patterns, thoroughly independent of one another. If this forms the foundation of a universal grammar, well and good.

Beyond that, it is unsafe to go. It is particularly unsafe to suppose, as did the Modistae, a basic morphological structure common to all languages, and based upon the grammatical categories and parts of speech of the Classical tongues.

It is interesting to speculate on how the error of universality could have arisen. Lack of observation, due to lack of interest, on the part of the ancients is undoubtedly one cause. Another is preoccupation with logic itself, the desire on the part of a people who were basically philosophers to bring order and law into a world in which order and law did not exist. Once we get into the Middle Ages, two variants of the same factors come into play. On the one hand, there is the fact that the tongues of medieval Europe, as of modern Europe, were nearly all of the Indo-European family, and thus rather easy to fit into the Classical mold, while other tongues with which the medieval Europeans were in contact were largely Semitic and Ural-Altaic, that is to say, of families whose structure does not diverge too widely from that of Indo-European. On the other hand, the concept of universality which had been created in the days of the glory of Rome had developed into the concept of a universal Church and a universal Empire, and it was not too difficult to transfer the concept of universality from the realm of religion and politics to that of linguistics. The concept of diversity, of national vernaculars and religious differences, came into being almost together with the western discovery of new, strange tongues of Asia, Africa and America which bore no structural resemblance to the familiar pattern.

But habits once formed are hard to break. Only traditionalism can account for the attempt to force all languages into the Graeco-Latin mold at a period when observation and inductive thinking were replacing "logical" deduction in a variety of realms. Certainly this was true by 1660, when the Port Royal Grammar appeared, with the subheading: *Les raisons de ce qui est commun à toutes les langues et des principales différences qui s'y rencontrent.*

Yet when the pendulum swung, it went perhaps too far in the opposite direction. Are we justified in denying all validity to the old grammatical concepts and categories? On a purely scientific basis, possibly so. On a practical basis, not quite.

The old grammatical concepts, categories and terminology, though originally derived from the Classical languages and based squarely on Indo-European, are nevertheless applicable, in slightly modified form, to the languages spoken by the majority of the world's inhabitants. Let us not forget, in this connection, that of the world's present population of about three billion, over half speak languages of the Indo-European family, and that if to this total we add languages of a somewhat similar structure, such as the Semitic and the Ural-Altaic, we come close to covering three-fourths of the world's people. This fact alone ought to give us pause before we decide to throw our old grammatical concepts into the scrap heap.

Secondly, there is the problem of replacement. Many of us view with some amusement (not unmixed with alarm) the attempts on the part of some linguists to evolve a set of concepts and terminologies that will cover the world situation as effectively as did the old ones. What they usually come out with is a multiplication of terms and concepts that can only bewilder and frustrate those who are exposed to them. It is particularly irritating to see these attempts being foisted upon languages where the old concepts and the old terminology fit the situation perfectly, or almost perfectly.

Perhaps the old universal grammar can still do practical service provided we remove the offending adjective "universal" and label it something else, and provided we do not try to apply it in the case of those languages where it is obviously out of place.

But for what concerns the true, scientific, objective universality of the grammatical concept and categories, the case is as hopeless as is the search for logic in language. There is no such thing as standardizing the human mind in the matter of linguistic expression. Each language is a law unto itself in the matter of what it considers logical, desirable or necessary.

A cursory examination of the situation existing in various tongues reveals two seemingly contradictory facts: 1. There is no such thing as universality of grammatical structure, even with allowance made for the accidental variations postulated by the Modistae; 2. In a great many cases, linguistic structures and modes of expression which at first glance seem completely dissimilar display, on careful analysis, surprising similarities of point of view and even form of expression, often with what is normal in one language appearing as an exception in another.

The chief grammatical categories set forth in the traditional manuals, and directly applicable to languages that partake of the ancient Indo-European structure, are the following: gender, number, case, person, tense, mood and voice. (The aspects of languages like the Slavic and Semitic may be viewed as an extension of both tense and mood, though they probably antedate both historically.) The traditional parts of speech are: article, noun, adjective, adverb, pronoun, verb, preposition, conjunction, interjection.

It may be noted that the grammatical concepts outlined above are in themselves logical and objective, since they reflect realities appearing in the external world (the opposition of animate to inanimate, or of male to female; the opposition of singleness to plurality; the doer vs. the receiver of an action; the speaker vs. the person addressed, or the person or thing spoken about; the time or fashion in which an occurrence takes place; the viewing of that occurrence as an actuality or a mere possibility; the person or thing mentioned performing or receiving the action; etc.). The only trouble with this "logical" segmentation of the universe is that it fails to take into account all the possibilities of external occurrence, and, conversely, that it includes some that may not necessarily be viewed as essential to a proper understanding of what it is desired to convey.

In like manner, the parts of speech reflect, quite faithfully, the formal distinctions of languages like Greek and Latin, and for these languages the distinctions are quite real and "logical," since the noun behaves differently from the adjective, and both differ in form and function from the verb. Again the trouble is that not all languages enjoy these distinctions, while others make further distinctions that must be taken into account.

Even where the languages are genetically related, strong points of divergence arise. One has only to reflect that of the two Classical languages one, Greek, has a definite article, while Latin does not; Quintilian's pronouncement, based on a comparison between Greek and Latin, is to the effect that *"nostra lingua articulum non desiderat"* ("our language does not desire an article"). On a broader front, many languages, of various families, deem it necessary to have the definite marker used with a noun that is specifically known; others, following Quintilian's example, reject it (in the Uralic group, for instance, Hungarian thinks a definite article is needed; Finnish does not). Where, then, is the universality, or even the logic, of the article?

The concept of grammatical gender works out differently in Greek, Latin, Sanskrit, German and Russian (where males are usually masculine, females are usually feminine, but inanimate objects are differently distributed among the three genders) from the way it works in Romance or Semitic (where there is no neuter gender, and inanimate objects are distributed among masculine and feminine), or in English (where inanimate objects are regularly called neuter, but a formal distinction of masculine, feminine and neuter appears only in the personal pronoun, and has vanished elsewhere). Many languages altogether reject the concept of grammatical gender, or replace it with the concept of caste, or of class of objects. Obviously, there is here no universality. As for logic, it all seems to depend on what type of logic you are using; or, to put it another way, on how you choose to segment the universe of your experience.

But here is where the contradiction sets in. Before we decide, on the basis of our own English speech-and-thought habits, that it is altogether illogical for Hungarian to use the same word for "he," "she" and "it," let us stop to reflect that in the plural form "they" we English speakers behave in exactly the same fashion, making no distinction whatsoever of animate or inanimate, male or female. Are French and Spanish more "logical" for having separate masculine and feminine forms for "they"? But then, are they not illogical when they use a masculine "they" for a group including both sexes?

The concept of grammatical number, of a distinction in form to separate "one" from "more than one," seems basic. Here Semitic, Greek and Sanskrit, with their dual number, remind us that there is another possible distinction of form that can be made. There is a possible logical justification for the dual, because many objects come normally in pairs (eyes, hands, feet, ears, to mention a few). Other little-known languages display special forms for three, four, and even more; we are satisfied with using the numeral before the name of the object. In still other languages, the concept of number is seldom expressed grammatically; if a distinction must be made, it is done by means of numerals, or of such words as "many," "various." Again, before we decide that this is altogether illogical, let us remember those limited words in English, like "sheep" and deer," where the plural has the same form as the singular. On the other hand, Chinese, which seldom bothers to add a plural suffix to nouns, invariably does so with its personal pronouns. As a grammatical concept, number seems to be neither universal nor logically treated.

For the grammatical concept of case, a perfect illustration of changing historical moods is supplied by the transition from Latin to the modern western Romance languages. In the latter, there is no trace of the old Latin separate case endings for nouns, and this permits some linguists to state that it is arrant nonsense to speak of nominative, genitive, dative, accusative and ablative in connection with Italian, French or Spanish. Yet all these languages display, in their personal pronouns, an almost perfect survival of separate case forms (Italian *egli,* nominative; *lo,* accusative; *gli,* dative; *lui,* ablative). Something similar appears in English, where the noun still shows a separate genitive case form ("the *boy's* book"), while the pronoun has at least three separate case forms (*I, my, me; he, his, him*). But there are languages, like Chinese, that do not have and seem never to have had anything even remotely resembling a case form, and indicate case relation exclusively by word order (*I see he; he see I;* and note the English parallel: *John sees Joe; Joe sees John*). The concept of case as a formal distinction is neither universal nor logical.

The idea of making a formal distinction between speaker, person addressed, and person or thing discussed is fundamental in some languages, unimportant in others, like Japanese, where the verb is impersonal. (*There-is-a-going* is the best literal translation for the form that does service for "I am going," "you are going," "he is going," etc.) Here the limited western parallel lies with such forms as French impersonal *on* ("*Où est-ce qu'on va?*"), and Italian or Spanish impersonal reflexive constructions ("*Dove si va stasera?*"). The Japanese, too, can personalize their verb by the use of a subject pronoun if they deem it necessary in order to avoid confusion; but this device is about as seldom employed as English *one* in "What is one to do?"

Even languages that regularly use person as a grammatical concept do not all handle it in the same fashion. Many distinguish between "inclusive" and "exclusive" *we* ("you and I," as against "he and I").

The contrast between tense and aspect is a basic illustration of the absence of universality and logic. Is it more logical to segment occurrences in accordance with time, or in accordance with whether the action is completed or incomplete? Or is it best to use a mixture of both, as Russian does? If time is the criterion, how many tenses are logically needed? Are present, past and future not enough? Is it necessary or desirable to indicate grammatically that an occurrence "had taken" place before another occurrence happened, or that something "will have taken" place by the time something else occurs? The number of languages that fail to distinguish time in the words that correspond to our verbs is large. Moods can range all the way from indicative, subjunctive, imperative and infinitive (and note that English and French have partly given up the subjunctive, at least in some tense forms) to the optative of Greek, the desiderative, causative, etc., of many other languages, and the utter lack of formal distinctions in a language like Chinese. For the voices, we have not only the active and passive of most western tongues, but also the middle of Greek (indicating that the subject acts upon himself, or in his own interest), and the reflexive which frequently replaces the passive in numerous languages.

Grammatical categories are neither universal nor logical. The traditional parts of speech, on the other hand, are beautifully suited to languages like Sanskrit, Greek, Latin, Russian, where each part of speech behaves in a characteristic way, but not so well suited to languages like English and Chinese, where the same word, without change in form, may assume a variety of grammatical functions. (*Mail* is a noun in "Put this letter in the mail"; an adjective in "Put this letter in the mailbox"; a verb in "Mail this letter"; *up* is a preposition in "I'm going up the river"; an adverb in "Going up"; a noun in "The ups and downs of life"; a verb in "I'll up you five dollars"; and it behaves like a compounded adjective in "uptown.") In other languages it is impossible to distinguish formally between a noun and a verb, or between a verb and an adjective.

Here again, however, we get strange parallels. Students of Far Eastern languages are at times surprised to find so-called "stative verbs" in Chinese (from the English standpoint, these are really words used as adjectives with the verb "to be" understood, as in *wǒ lèi,* "I tired," for "I am tired"); but Indo-European Russian does precisely the same thing in the present tense (*ya rad,* "I glad," for "I am glad"); they are also surprised to find "adjectives conjugated like verbs" in Japanese (*shiroi,* "white," but also "to be white"; *shirokatta,* "was white"); yet in Italian *biancheggiare,* "to gleam white," formed on the root of *bianco,* "white," works in practically the same way.

Other striking language diversities, with logical implications, come to mind. In the matter of a demonstrative adjective, English distinguishes between what is near the speaker ("this," "these") and what is removed from him ("that," "those"); Spanish makes a threefold distinction (*este, ese aquel*) between what is near the speaker, what is near the person addressed, and what is removed from both (English used to have the same threefold distinction by the use of "yon" for what is removed from both speaker and person addressed, but gave it up as unnecessary); French does not normally bother to distinguish at all (*ce livre,* "this book" or "that book"), though the distinction can be made if felt to be necessary (*ce livre-ci, ce livre-là*). Some languages have as many as five or six demonstrative adjectives for varying degrees of remoteness (what is past, what is out of sight, etc.).

In inflected languages, the matter of agreement shows a surprising variety of frames of mind. The Romance languages, though they have given up the Latin cases for nouns, still find it expedient to demonstrate gender and number with all forms associated with the noun (articles, adjectives, demonstratives, possessives, etc.). English does not feel that this is at all necessary ("the good girl," where there is no formal indication of gender or number in "the" or "good," vs. Spanish *la buena muchacha,* where feminine gender and singular number are indicated in each word). German experiences the need for an elaborate formal distinction based on whether the adjective is preceded by another word that bears indication of number, gender and case (*der gute Mann* vs. *ein guter Mann*), but deems agreement unnecessary if a predicate adjective is involved (*der Mann ist gut*). Russian, with an elaborate set of agreements for both attributive and predicate adjectives, throws up the sponge if the adjective is in the comparative degree, and makes it invariable. Nothing could be more illogical or complicated than the rules for agreement of the past participle in French and Italian, and Spanish deserves a medal for having thrown out such rules and made the participle invariable (with a single "logical" exception: if the participle follows "to be" and may therefore be viewed as an adjective).

While it is perfectly true that for these and many other divergences among languages there are historical explanations ("causes" is perhaps too strong a word to use), it is undeniable that both universality and logic are absent from the language picture. Even constructed languages like Esperanto are highly illogical and altogether arbitrary in their structure, however the latter may have been "simplified."

This is not to say that we should throw out our grammatical categories and parts of speech, which can still do service in a majority of instances. It only means that we must be more elastic in our thinking and not try to apply them blindly in those cases where they obviously do not apply.

Yet the twin problems of universality and logic in language continue to fascinate many linguists and students of language. It is not only descriptivists like De Saussure and structuralists like Martinet[6] and quasi-mathematicians like Hjelmslev[7] who endeavor to create a new linguistic universality and logic in grammatical concepts, but also members of the American anthropological school of linguistics whose basic proposition is language diversity and the necessity for studying each language in a vacuum. Most spectacular among the latter, by reason of his attempt to explore anew the problem of a universal grammar, is B. L. Whorf, whose untimely death prevented him from carrying on his studies to more definite conclusions.[8]

NOTES TO PROBLEM II

1. Robins, *op. cit.,* p. 21.
2. Robins, *op. cit.,* p. 26.
3. Robins, *op. cit.,* p. 40.
4. Robins, *op. cit.,* p. 77.

5. J. Descartes, *Lettre au Père Mersenne* (Nov. 20, 1629), ed. Adam-Tannery, I, pp. 76–79, Paris, 1898.

6. A. Martinet, *Economie des changements phonétiques,* Paris, 1955.

7. L. Hjelmslev, *Principes de grammaire générale,* Copenhagen, 1928, pp. 15, 268ff.

8. See chapters "Grammatical Categories" and "Language: Plan and Conception of Arrangement," in *Language, Thought and Reality,* ed. J. B. Carroll, Cambridge, 1956. See also V. Brøndal, *Les Parties du Discours,* Copenhagen, 1948; L. H. Gray, *op. cit.,* chapters "The Parts of Speech," "The Grammatical Categories," pp. 144–223.

Law or Free Choice?

AS FAR back as the fifth century B.C., early Greek grammarians engaged in controversy as to whether language functions by "analogy" or "anomaly." Can the facts of grammar be made more systematic than they appear in observed usage? Or should what is actually observed, however anomalous or unsystematic, be accepted and sanctioned?[1] Insofar as this question applies to language as handled by its speakers, it may be said to form part of another, related problem, to be discussed later.

But there is another way of viewing the analogy-anomaly controversy, and that is as applied to language itself, independently of the way it may be handled or mishandled by individuals. Does language submit to certain specific laws, or is it a creature of whim, developing and changing in haphazard fashion?

It is particularly with reference to *changing* language that this last question comes up. The ancients, if they gave any mind to the problem of language change (there is some evidence that they were at least aware of it),[2] carefully avoided combining their observations with the issue. Their general unspoken attitude was that language ought to stay fixed.

The Middle Ages and the Renaissance could not avoid the problem, by reason of the increasing wealth of observable material. The mere existence of vernaculars derived from Latin meant that change in language had to be accepted and considered, and, as a matter of fact, it was discussed by writers like Dante and Valdés.[3]

When it came to describing in some orderly fashion the changes that had occurred in the observable languages, the situation was lamentable. Even where etymologies were half properly presented, as in the work of Ménage,[4] no satisfactory attempt was made to draw from the examples described any general statements as to the way in which the changes had taken place. It was not until the beginning of the nineteenth century that the combined work of Schlegel, Rask, Bopp, Grimm and, later, Verner brought some order out of chaos. These scholars set the beginning of the so-called comparative method, whereby, after laying side by side a number of suitable examples, one could confidently assert that if a certain Indo-European root developed with an initial p in Sanskrit, Greek, Latin and Slavic, one could expect an f in the Germanic equivalent, an h in the Armenian, and fall of the initial consonant in Celtic. Inspired by the example of these early workers in the comparative field, Friedrich Diez undertook to perform the same operation for the development of the Romance languages from Latin.[5] (He had a far easier task, since Latin supplied him with a known starting point for the language changes, something that the workers in the general Indo-European field had lacked.)

So far there had been no controversy, but only co-operation among the linguists. But in 1876 A. Leskien, in his *Deklination im Slavisch-Litauischen und Germanischen,* formulated a general principle of linguistic change which was quickly picked up by other distinguished scholars, notably Brugmann and Osthoff. The principle, briefly stated, is that "all sound change, insofar as it proceeds mechanically, takes place in accordance with laws which know no exception (*nach ausnahmlosen Gesetzen*)."

Others were quick to point out that there were plenty of exceptions. The *Junggrammatiker*, or Neogrammarians, as the proponents of the *Lautgesetz* styled themselves, quickly replied with statements that in part sound like hedging: the exceptionless change, for one thing, must occur in a given area and at a given period, since the law operative for one dialectal zone need not apply to another, and the operation of the law is definitely circumscribed in time, so that a word entering the language after the law has ceased operating is not subject to that law. This would mean that a word coming, let us say, into French from Italian, or from the Picard dialectal area, or from learned Latin, can not be taken as an illustration of the functioning or nonfunctioning of the law. (The general law of French development for free stressed Latin *a* is that it turns into *e*, as illustrated by *amare* to *aimer*, *mare* to *mer*, etc. *Rarum* should then give *rer*, not *rare;* but *rare* is a learned word, brought from book Latin into French long after the law ceased to operate. In like manner, *soldat* [Latin *soldatum*] comes into French from Italian, and *cap* [Latin *caput, capum*] from Provençal; the native French developments call for *soudé* and *chef;* both actually appear, with different meanings.)

A second valid line of defense for the believers in the sound law was provided by the fact that laws are sometimes incorrectly or incompletely stated. Verner had already spectacularly demonstrated this in presenting his famous law, which is in the nature of an exception to Grimm's Law for the Germanic consonant shifts; but the exceptions occur under very specific conditions; and Verner had stated at the time that "where there is an apparent irregularity there must be a rule for irregularity; the problem is to find it."

But after all foreign, learned and dialectal borrowings, real or fancied, had been taken into account, and all regular exceptions to the rules of sound change, occurring under specific conditions, had been formulated, there still remained a rather large residuum of exceptions to the laws. Here the Lautgesetzers invoked another principle which, by its very nature, was difficult to contradict, the principle of change by analogy. Analogy in linguistics may be defined as imitation by one word of another word with which it has a real or fancied affiliation; the word which submits to such analogy thereby makes its escape from the working of the iron-bound law. (To exemplify: since Latin stressed long *i*, in all positions, gives rise to *i* in both French and Italian, *frīgidum* should have come out as *frid* in French and *friddo* in Italian; it does come out as *frío* in Spanish. The fact that it fails to have its expected outcome in French and Italian, and shows instead in *froid* and *freddo* a development that could come from short *i*, but not from long *i*, is alleged to be due to the constant association of the word for "cold" with *rigidum,* "stiff," which has a short stressed *i*. This is plausible, but not scientifically demonstrable. The French -*ons* ending in the first person plural of verbs, instead of a variety of other endings which the Latin originals would lead us to expect, is said to be due to widespread analogy with Old French *sons* from Latin *sumus,* a form which itself later disappeared in the face of the competition of *sommes* from a Vulgar Latin *summus.* Again, this is quite plausible, but not susceptible of absolute proof.)

Analogy being, by its very nature, a highly elastic and flexible line of defense, it was not only adroitly used, but maladroitly overused by the believers in the sound laws. But analogy and kindred phenomena, such as metathesis, assimilation and dissimilation, are observed to work so capriciously, so haphazardly, that they often give comfort to the opponents of the sound law rather than to its supporters.

In spite of all the exceptions, however, it is undeniable that the laws of sound change are in the main operative. If one is willing to forego comparing them to the laws of physics or chemistry and accept instead comparison with the man-made laws of the political world (language is, after all, a human, not a metallic activity), one could then say that the sound law is obeyed by the majority of forms, just as statute law is obeyed by the majority of citizens; but that there are a number of forms and persons who violate both. If the word "tendency" is used to replace "law," a better picture of the actual situation seems to result.

Many noted linguists opposed the sound-law theory at the time of its formulation and for decades thereafter. Among them may be mentioned G. Curtius, K. Vossler, H. Schuchardt, G. I. Ascoli, G. Bertoni and M. Bartoli, whose *Introduzione alla neolinguistica* (1925) summarizes the anti-Neogrammarian point of view. The stand of the Neolinguists, as this group called itself, is that sound changes are sporadic and individualistic phenomena, conditioned by the factor of dialects (in the final analysis, these are as numerous as the speakers), and by linguistic substrata and superstrata. Schuchardt holds that languages do not exist in a vacuum, and that innovations are created by individuals and extended to the group, with pockets of resistance and long periods of transition.[6]

It may be mentioned in passing that there are some (but these are usually philosophers rather than linguists) who deny all validity to the sound laws or even to the sound tendencies, and prefer to view all language change as occurring at random. These ultramentalists are perhaps as unreasonable in their stand as the ultramechanists. The facts speak for themselves.

What are these facts? To deny the existence of a tendency on the part of language sounds to change uniformly, within the bounds and with the exceptions already noted, is irrational. To seek an explanation for every apparent exception is not only human, but scientifically praiseworthy. To create analogical explanations out of thin air and try to palm them off on the unsuspecting public as gospel truth is both unscientific and dishonest. Yet this is precisely what was done over a considerable period of time by many supposedly reputable scholars, particularly in the field of Romance development.

Again, there are certain languages where the "laws" seem to work with reasonable accuracy, others where the establishment of definite laws in certain sound changes appears well-nigh impossible. (The law of syncopation of post-tonic vowels, for example, works with almost clocklike regularity in French, much less definitely in Spanish, in approximately half the cases in Italian; the same may be said for the diphthongization of free short *e* and short *o,* for the -*e* outcome of Latin short -*e,* long -*e* and short -*i* in the final syllable; and for half a dozen other major phenomena).[7] The question then arises: which is the "regular," which the "exceptional" outcome? Shall we take a poll of forms, and base our conclusion on a slender majority, as in the Kennedy-Nixon election? Or try to settle the issue on the basis that the two conflicting outcomes represent two different dialectal tendencies? If so, where is our evidence? And if we invoke dialectal merger, what then happens to the other theory, so dear to the heart of the mechanists, that Italian is the Florentine dialect pure and simple, and not a conglomeration of dialects, as Dante himself suggested?[8]

There is no doubt that for every effect there is a cause. The difficulty, as Verner pointed out, is in finding the appropriate cause for each effect. But when both effects and causes multiply to such a degree that one has to set up an endless table of special laws to justify visible exceptions to the main law, then the question becomes cogent whether it is possible to speak of a "law" in the generally accepted sense of the word.

It is the vogue among historical linguists today, insofar as there are any historical linguists left in this new world of descriptivism and structuralism, to take it for granted that the victory in the long-drawn-out controversy rests with the proponents of the sound law, always with the proviso that the numerous extraneous factors listed above are taken into consideration. This is begging the question. The *Lautgesetz* is far from being left in control of the battlefield. The exceptions are far too numerous, and too many of them are not explainable by any sort of reasonable device tending to place them in neat pigeonholes.

There is only one rational way to face this problem, and that is to admit that under no circumstances can the laws of language change be said to have the cogency of the laws of physics. (Note, by the way, that since Einsteinian relativity appeared, physical scientists are no longer cocksure about the universal validity of the laws of Newtonian physics.)

Language is a product of the human mind, not something mechanical. The human mind notoriously rejects universal regimentation, although it is quite possible, for limited periods of time, to make most people behave and think in the same way. But at the very time and in the very area where a transformation in human thought is occurring, there is always a nonconformist group that evades the law. The same thing happens in language. Far from the transformation being universal in the same period over a given area, direct observation shows that it is perfectly possible to have two or more different pronunciations (usually one more conservative, the other an innovation) which coexist for years, occasionally for centuries. The two possible pronunciations of English *tomato* and *either* are clear cases in point. Other clear-cut examples: the fact that in the eleventh-century French of the *Chanson de Roland, ai* is in assonance half the time with *a*, the other half with *e*, clearly indicating that it could be pronounced as either [aj] or [ɛ] ;[9] the fact that the abortive fifteenth-century movement to change French *r* to *z* failed to go through in the majority of instances, but did go through in a few forms, *chaise* from an earlier *chaire* among them, and that both words survive to the present day. Other proofs of the coexistence of two pronunciations, one older, the other an innovation, are French *François* and *Français, roide* and *raide,* both pairs stemming from the same source.

In conclusion, the problem of law vs. free choice must be solved on a compromise basis, with the recognition of trends or tendencies in linguistic change, accompanied by numerous exceptions, many of which are reducible to secondary laws, while others must be described as exceptions pure and simple, due to the capricious arbitrium of the speakers (influenced, no doubt, by a specific cause at the time they exercised their arbitrium). The factual reality of double outcomes for which there is no clear-cut explanation on the basis of borrowing or analogy must also be faced. But these realities do not invalidate the other reality of a trend or tendency in language change.

After all, why expect, in a human, sociological activity like language, that one hundred per cent unanimity which not even the tightest forms of dictatorship are able to achieve?

NOTES TO PROBLEM III

1. Robins, *op. cit.,* p. 16.

2. Polybius (*Hist.* III, 22), speaking of a treaty between Rome and Carthage, composed probably in 507 B.C., states that the language used in that document, four centuries before his time, is so different from the tongue of his own day that even the most learned scholars have difficulty

in interpreting it. Five centuries later, St. Jerome (*Pauli Epistola ad Galatas*, II, Foreword), says "cum . . . et ipsa latinitas et regionibus quotidie mutetur et tempore" ("since the Latin language itself changes daily, both in space and in time"). See Monteverdi, *op. cit.*, pp. 17, 47.

3. Dante, *De Vulgari Eloquentia*, 1305; J. de Valdés, *Diálogo de la lengua*, 1533.

4. G. Ménage, *Origines de la langue française*, 1650.

5. F. Diez, *Grammatik der romanischen Sprachen*, 1836–1844.

6. For the history of the great controversy, see Iordan and Orr, *op. cit.*, pp. 86–143. See also H. Paul, *Prinzipien der Sprachwissenschaft*, 1880, for a summation of the Neogrammarian point of view.

7. See M. Pei, *The Italian Language*, New York, 1941, pp. 31, n. 3; 35; 38–39; M. Pei, "Di un doppio esito fonetico italiano," *Lingua Nostra*, III, 1 (1942), pp. 8–9; M. Pei, "Latin and Italian Front Vowels," *Modern Language Notes*, LVIII, 2 (Feb. 1943), pp. 116–120.

8. R. A. Hall, Jr., review of M. Pei, *The Italian Language*, in *Language* 17.3. 263–9 (July-Sept. 1941); *The Italian 'Questione della Lingua*,' Chapel Hill, 1942.

9. For a different interpretation of this phenomenon (that the Oxford manuscript is a conglomeration of manuscripts of different periods), see R. A. Hall, Jr., *Romance Philology* XIII (1959–1960), p. 156. Hall's line of reasoning is characteristic of the mentality of true believers in the sound law; if the documentary evidence doesn't fit your theory, throw away the evidence, not the theory.

Monogenesis or Polygenesis?

THE problem of a single or plural origin for the world's languages was rather quickly and neatly disposed of by the ancients. Since each group regarded its own language as the only one worthy of the name, it stood to reason that that language was the original one, and all others were derived from it, if, indeed, one could speak of derivation in connection with mere babblings. On the Hebrew side, the Biblical account of the rise of diversity among the languages is clearly monogenetic, and the reasons for divergence from the original prototype are openly attributed to man's own pride and instinct for disobedience. Indians and Greeks did not trouble to discuss language diversity. Both sides in the discussion embodied in Plato's *Cratylus* make it abundantly clear that whatever they have to say concerning the origin of language applies to the Greek language and no other. The Romans, somewhat painfully aware of Greek, hinted that their own language was descended from it.

The Middle Ages, with their stress upon the things of the next world, implicitly and literally followed the Biblical story of the

Tower of Babel. Hebrew was therefore the original tongue, and all others somehow stemmed from it. Dante, straddling the Middle Ages and the Renaissance, correctly traced the Romance languages back to Latin, but carefully refrained from advancing any theories as to where Latin itself might have come from. It was not until the sixteenth century, when many strange and remote tongues had come to the notice of the West, that the question of classification and affiliation began to be discussed; but the issue of monogenesis or polygenesis was still carefully eschewed, possibly because it would have involved its formulator in a religious controversy. As late as the seventeenth century it was common for amateur linguists to derive Latin, Greek and vernacular words from Hebrew or "Chaldean," by a simple process of adding, subtracting, transposing or inverting letters.[1] Similar unscientific pronouncements about the historical priority of certain languages go on being made even today, but no one pays any serious attention to them.

Rather poor attempts at the classification of languages now known to belong to different families had been made in 1548 by T. Bibliander,[2] in 1555 by C. Gesner,[3] and by J. J. Scaliger in 1599.[4] All of them skirted the problem of monogenesis. Now came G. W. von Leibniz, with his *Brevis Designatio Meditationum de Originibus Gentium Ductis Potissimum ex Indiciis Linguarum* (1710), to suggest the existence of a protospeech or protospeeches antedating historical records; but he, too, failed to pose squarely the question of monogenesis.

The religious tradition on the one hand, the belief in a universal grammar on the other, combined to postpone any scientific discussion of the problem until after the discovery of the unity of the Indo-European languages at the beginning of the nineteenth century. At that time, the question of monogenesis was temporarily settled, not so much by argument as by default. If the Indo-

European tongues were definitely and demonstrably linked, then other languages with which the link could not be established by the same methods were evidently of a different origin. This point of view so thoroughly replaced, at least in scientific circles, the earlier belief that all languages stemmed from Hebrew, that throughout most of the nineteenth century, the century of historical linguistics par excellence, there is not even a good discussion of the problem, one way or the other.

By the beginning of the twentieth century, the question appeared settled. Most languages had been classified and pigeonholed in a more or less satisfactory fashion: Indo-European, Semito-Hamitic, Ural-Altaic, Sino-Tibetan, Dravidian, Japanese-Korean, Malayo-Polynesian, Bantu, and so forth. Any linguist who might have been interviewed on this specific topic: "Do you believe that all of the world's languages stem from a single prototype, or do you hold that the various language families arose independently of one another in various parts of the earth?" would either have refused to answer on grounds of self-incrimination, or would have conveniently referred you to his fellow-scientists, the anthropologists.

This is not so absurd or evasive a procedure as one might think. The implication is quite clear: the problem of monogenesis in language is definitely linked with the problem of monogenesis of man himself. If the human race first arose, whether by creation or by evolution, in a single spot, and later wandered off in different directions, giving rise to mankind's assorted and picturesque races, it could logically be assumed that language was bestowed upon it, or was first evolved by it, in the place of its origin, and that the later migrations and infinite diversifications of man were attended by similar infinite diversifications in man's language. If, on the other hand, human groups arose in different localities, each with its own characteristics, then it is equally logical to suppose that each group evolved its own speech forms independently of the others, save insofar as later contacts might have led to borrowings of words and forms.

Now the monogenesis of the human race is one problem on which anthropologists are noticeably and understandably discreet. Their reluctance to make categorical pronouncements is no longer based on fears of running into religious reprisals at the hands of those who interpret the Bible literally, but on lack of satisfactory evidence, in either direction. Darwin, in his *Descent of Man,*[5] made a somewhat cautious statement to the effect that despite certain dissimilarities of color, hair, shape of skull, etc., the structural resemblances among the various races are such as to justify belief in descent from a common species. But the evidence is far from one hundred per cent conclusive. Other anthropologists have pointed to the fact that the white race is found at its purest around the shores of the Baltic, the yellow at the bend of the Hoang Ho, the black in the region of the Gulf of Guinea, and that racial characteristics become more and more diluted as we move away from these focal centers.[6] This would certainly seem to indicate three separate points of origin for human beings and, by implication, for their languages.

Polygenesis of language, tentatively accepted in the course of the nineteenth century for lack of evidence to the contrary, found its most outspoken opponent in the person of A. Trombetti, who in his *Unità d'origine del linguaggio* (Bologna, 1905), and later, in his *Elementi di glottologia* (Bologna, 1922–1923), upheld the thesis of the original unity of all languages. Trombetti was criticized on the score that despite the immense amount of material he had gathered, he was led by superficial resemblances and ill-founded theories to conclusions incommensurate in value with the labor expended.[7]

But perhaps what could not be accomplished by a single stroke of genius may yet be attained by painstaking, point-by-point comparison among various supposedly independent language families.

There is some evidence of a possible link between Indo-European and Semito-Hamitic;[8] between Indo-European and Uralic;[9] between Munda, Mon-Khmer, Malayo-Polynesian, Sino-Tibetan, Uralic and Australian;[10] between Semito-Hamitic and Bantu.[11]

If these links are ever definitely established (and it will take a great deal of very hard work to establish them in the form of fully acceptable evidence) the case for monogenesis will be at least half proved. For the time being, the only attitude that the linguist can adopt is one of watchful reserve. But watchful reserve does not mean outright skepticism, or a refusal to look at the available evidence, as, if and when it unfolds.

NOTES TO PROBLEM IV

1. See, for instance, E. Guichard, *Harmonie étymologique des langues,* Paris, 1606.

2. *De Ratione Communi Omnium Linguarum et Litterarum Commentarius,* Zürich.

3. *Mithridates,* Zürich.

4. *Diatriba de Europaeorum Linguis.*

5. Chapter VII.

6. R. Benedict and G. Weltfish, *Races of Mankind,* New York, Public Affairs Committee, 1943. See also R. Benedict, *Race, Science and Politics,* New York, Viking, 1959.

7. Gray, *op. cit.,* p. 454. For another unfavorable evaluation of Trombetti's point of view, see H. Schuchardt, *Brevier,* 1928, p. 258. Schuchardt believes in a nonhistorical "elementary kinship" (based upon the fundamental resemblance of human mental processes) of languages for which there is no evidence of mutual relationship or historical contact. This only leads us back to the anthropologists.

8. H. Möller, *Semitisch und Indogermanisch,* Copenhagen, 1907; *Vergleichendes indogermanisch-semitisches Wörterbuch,* Göttingen, 1911; A. Cuny, *Etudes prégrammaticales sur le domaine des langues indoeuropéennes et chamito-sémitiques,* Paris, 1924.

9. B. Collinder, *Indo-uralisches Sprachgut,* Upsala, 1934.

10. Gray, *op. cit.,* p. 393.

11. Gray, *op. cit.,* p. 406.

Language, Race, Nationality and Religion

THE only valid reason for linking together under one heading the four items that appear in the title of this chapter is that they possess a least common denominator of intolerance and fanaticism, founded upon a basic misunderstanding of each and every one of them.

Throughout recorded history, we see men fighting, killing and dying in the name of one or another of these slogan words. To them may be added a fifth slogan, class, though an attempt to link language with social or economic class has appeared only in modern times, and in Soviet circles.[1]

Racial wars, in a broad sense, are perhaps inherent in the human being, as are wars among the species and subspecies of the animal kingdom. Two primitive groups that come in contact will often, though not necessarily, clash. If they speak different languages, the clash may easily result from misunderstanding of one another's intentions, though just as often hostile intentions precede linguistic incomprehension. It is this feature, by the way, that leads proponents of international, universal tongues to advertise their products on the basis of the theory that "understanding" (a much belabored word) will inevitably lead to peace, love and universal brotherhood. But Cain and Abel enjoyed perfect linguistic understanding; so did the followers of Marius and Sulla, of Pompey and Caesar, of Marc Antony and Octavian; so did the Confederates and the Unionists of the American Civil War, the Bolsheviks and Tsarists of the Russian, the Falangists and Loyalists of the Spanish.

The idea of an inherent link between race and language may have its inception in fact, in the sense that races in their aboriginal state may have spoken totally indigenous and different languages. (This would be true if polygenesis rather than monogenesis is accepted.) But historical circumstances are such as to dissolve, almost inevitably and universally, the link that may have existed at the outset. Nobody in his sound mind believes that today only people of Nordic body structure speak Indo-European languages. Even if this was once the case, the lineal descendants of the original Indo-European speech have today become the property of so many different racial groups, including, to cite a few glaring examples, American Negroes in the U.S.A., American Indians throughout North, Central and South America, brown-skinned Hawaiians and yellow-skinned Nisei and American-born Chinese, that the issue of a link between race and language has ceased to exist. There may be a basis of logic and fact in racial strife, though not a very good one, in this writer's opinion. There may also be a basis of logic and fact in purely linguistic strife, like the language riots among people of the same race and religion, but endowed with different language backgrounds, that have recently delighted India, East Pakistan and Ceylon. But there is no basis of logic or fact in a conflict based on an attempt to merge the two factors. Even the Nazis, with their racial theories, stepped rather lightly on the language issue; they realized that Jews and other races they deemed inferior often spoke languages as Indo-European as their own, and perhaps more flawlessly.

The link between language and religion is at best a shadowy one. Religion may have a specified language as its carrier (Hebrew served Judaism in that role, Arabic served Islam, Greek and Latin served Christianity) but ordinarily religion seeks to convert, and the medium of conversion is secondary. Only occasionally does a linguistic form function as a religious shibboleth. India's religious wars, at the time of partition and before, held little linguistic content.

We are perhaps oversimplifying the picture, in view of the subtle distinctions between Urdu and Hindi, Cyrillic and Roman script, different wordings in the Protestant and Catholic Bibles, and other such debatable issues. But it is nevertheless true that very seldom if at all does the factor of language loom paramount in connection with religious belief or religious intolerance.

When we come to that third, comparatively modern, still slightly confused factor known as nationality, or national consciousness, language often assumes a primary role. The concept of national loyalty, as separate from loyalty to an individual ruler or a dynasty, is a highly complex sociological phenomenon, in which race, religion and language may all play a part, or from which they may all be practically absent. Centralized governments, once they are established, often, though not invariably, tend to favor a centralized language, which will facilitate their work of standardization and uniformity of thinking; but there are many examples of national states which are strong despite language diversity (Switzerland and Belgium are two cases in point).

India and Pakistan based their separate nationhood primarily on the religious factor, then found linguistic diversity rising up to plague them. The recent history of France and Spain shows attempts at linguistic uniformity, with religious and racial factors thrust into the background; but there was an earlier period in Spanish and French history when religious uniformity was paramount, and both language and race took a back seat. Hitler's Germany tried to use the racial yardstick to measure national unity. Communist countries, at least officially, view language, religion and race as unimportant, and attempt to base their concept of nationhood on social class. Democracies of the American type endeavor to make no legal distinction of race, religion or social class, but give some official prominence to the language factor, at least to the extent of declaring the English language official and making its study compulsory throughout the American school system.

The ancients displayed mixed standards. Race and religion counted little, language was paramount, but only insofar as it was linked with a concept of universality and a complete way of life. The Hebrews were perhaps the only people of antiquity who welded the concepts of race, religion and language into a homogenized unit. The Greeks spread their language culturally, for the most part. The Romans spread theirs as part of a broader program and concept of general Romanization. There are no ancient accounts of persecutions or wars based primarily on the linguistic factor. A linguistic form could on occasion function as a shibboleth; but it was only symbolical of something else.

The Middle Ages have much to offer in the way of religious, dynastic and feudal wars, little in the way of linguistic intolerance or conflict. In western Europe, Latin was viewed as the universal language of scholarship, religion, diplomacy, and everything outside of purely colloquial interchange; and for the latter, broad freedom and tolerance seem to have prevailed.

As the vernaculars turned literary and grew in court and courtly use, however, one has the feeling that the new spirit of nationalism was at least in part founded on the factor of language. As each language emerged, each nation began to feel itself a nation, in the modern sense. When disparaging statements about foreign languages begin to appear, as in Olivier Basselin's satire on the speech of the English who were trying to make themselves the masters of France in the Hundred Years' War, the link between language and nationality appears established in the popular mind.

Language comparisons, too, make their appearance, with the writers of each country normally extolling their own native tongues. Only occasionally do we have a tribute to an alien tongue of the type of Brunetto Latini's thirteenth-century statement that "the speech of the French is more delectable and common to all men."

From the fourteenth century on, each country regales us with panegyrics concerning its own language. The implication of a link between language and nationality, or nationalism, is clear.

The idea of establishing a scientifically definite link between language and the mentality, psychology or behavior pattern of the speaking group seems to originate with Leibniz who, in the late seventeenth century, maintained that language is the mirror of a nation's spiritual life. This thought was continued and expanded by W. von Humboldt, who in his *Ueber die Kawisprache* (1836–1837) formulated the theory that language is the outer manifestation of a people's soul, and even the creator of their pattern of thought. This intimate link between language and the psychology of the nation or speaking group had been advanced at an earlier date, but by philosophers who were not primarily linguists (G. B. Vico, and particularly Herder, *Ueber den Ursprung der Sprache,* 1772). Later proponents were K. Vossler, with his "national genius," E. Lerch, with his theory that the national attitude leads to linguistic creation, and Grammont, who believes that the differences between German and English, two languages that sprang from a common source, are to be explained in terms of the psychological differences between the two peoples. Twentieth-century opposition is voiced, among others, by De Saussure and Vendryes, who refuse to admit that there is any connection between the development of a language and the mentality of the people who speak it.[2]

The latest variant of this problem is supplied by Whorf who, going back in part to the ideas of Humboldt, reverses the terms of the controversy by claiming that it is the language that influences the psychology of the ethnic group rather than the opposite. We are influenced in our mode of thinking and our behavior, says Whorf, by the type of language we habitually speak. A language whose verb has clear and precise tense distinctions, for instance, will induce in its speakers a keen consciousness of time values and punctuality, while a language in which the action is represented merely as occurring, without reference to time, will create in its speakers a sense of timelessness that will lead them to shrug their shoulders at time clocks and due dates.

To summarize, the link between language and race may perhaps be admitted in origin, but is today largely meaningless, by reason of the wholesale adoptions of once alien languages by both individuals and groups, as well as by reason of the tremendous racial minglings that have occurred historically.

The link between language and religion is admissible to the same extent that we can allow for other important sociological factors. Religious belief leads to linguistic creation, linguistic borrowing, and numerous other linguistic processes. But so do trade, war, politics, science, social phenomena of all descriptions. The link is historical and specific, not inherent and universal.

The point that really remains to be settled is whether there is an inherent link between language and nationality, or, to put it more exactly, between language and the mentality of the ethnic group. If the link is accepted (and here linguistic opinion is strongly divided, and powerful arguments can be advanced both ways), then a secondary problem arises: is it mainly language that influences psychology and behavior, as sustained in modern times by Whorf and his followers, or is it the ethnic mentality that influences language, as held by all of Whorf's predecessors from Leibniz down to the present, with the possible exception of Humboldt?

The answer to the first question hinges largely upon the viewpoint of the individual. It is no accident that followers of the mechanistic school of linguistics (those who hold that language change, language learning, and language itself are mechanical, automatic, reflex processes, in which the conscious mind plays little or no part) reject the link between language and ethnic mentality, while the mentalistic school (and this includes philosophers as well as linguists) implicitly believes in the connection.

If the link is accepted, the implications are fascinating. We can then not only explain past language change in terms of the way a group thinks and behaves (Grammont, for example, says that despite their common origin, English has become a commonplace idiom, *"plate et terre à terre,"* while German is a language with a rich vocabulary, but lacking the finer shades, and full of useless complications; how else, he asks, are we to explain this phenomenon than by the mentality of the respective peoples?); we can also to some extent prophesy the direction that future evolution of each language will take. (American English, for instance, will become still more materialistic, commercialized, direct, lacking in grace and refinement, while at the same time multiplying ad infinitum both its scientific and its slang vocabulary, while British English will remain far more conservative, precise, and polysyllabic; Italian and Spanish will become even more mellifluous, euphonic, pompous and circumlocutory than they are today, while Russian will throw off the shackles of its rigid case endings and extremely long words and shape itself into a tough, resilient language fit for propaganda and proletarian use.)

But is it really so? Above all, does the ethnic mentality remain the same, or does it change in accordance with external historical conditions? Do the present-day Italians think like the ancient Romans, or like the Florentines of the Renaissance, or is their line of thought completely different? Are the quiet, rational Frenchmen of today the roistering French of the days of Villon and d'Artagnan? Are the present-day Americans who have to ride to battle in jeeps the same hardy breed as the pioneers who opened up the West? What the mentalists seem to forget is that ethnic mentalities and ethnic forms of behavior change to approximately the same degree as language, so that the relation between the two, if one exists, is between two variables, not two constants, or even a variable and a constant.

A point-by-point examination of any given language will probably reveal as many features in disagreement as in agreement with what could be described as the psychology of the speaking group (always granting that we can describe the psychology of an entire group, particularly a large, national group). In this, as in many other problems, linguistic and otherwise, it is easy for us to sort out from the available evidence what supports our preconceived point of view and neglect everything else. So far, that is all that has been done.

A truly scientific investigation of the problem would call for: 1. an evaluation and description, at least reasonably approximate, of national psychological traits; to isolate a minimum of such traits that even a mere majority of the judges would accept as valid would be a well-nigh impossible task; 2. a study of the features of the language, to decide what psychological significance each one has (again an almost insurmountable task) ; 3. placing the language features in juxtaposition with the psychological traits, and making sure that the ones illustrate the others. Only then will we begin to approach a solution of the problem. It goes without saying that the grammatical or phonological or lexical traits that do not fit into any psychological pigeonhole are not to be discarded, but retained and carefully weighed against the positive evidence. So far, no one has undertaken such a study, and in the nature of things it is extremely doubtful that anyone ever will.

There remains the secondary question whether group mentality influences language, language influences group mentality, or each influences the other. (This question, by the way, is really valid only if the link between language and group psychology and behavior is at least tentatively accepted.)

Here, the evidence for the influence of the speakers' environment and activities upon their language is historically attested, abundant and incontrovertible, particularly for what concerns vocabulary. This is not at all the same as saying that the language is influenced by the speakers' basic mentality or psychology, for the latter would normally antedate their environment and activities. Environment and activities are fully measurable, while mentality and psychology, particularly for a large group, are not.

There is little and doubtful evidence of the contrary phenomenon, the influence of language upon environment and activities. Of course, once the language is established, it must act as the descriptive vehicle for the group's work and behavior. It is even possible that by reason of its descriptive and analytical powers, the language may, in conjunction with other factors, stimulate the growth of new activities. But some form of environment and activity must precede the language that describes them. If the Hopi Indian views and segments his universe differently from the white man, it is not because his language compels him to do so, but because his experience is different. Thought and language, after all, reflect the world of our experience. But the world of our experience is all too often beyond the control of either our thought or our language.

NOTES TO PROBLEM V

1. See J. V. Murra, R. M. Hankin and F. Holling, *The Soviet Linguistic Controversy,* New York, King's Crown Press, 1951. N. Y. Marr, a prominent Soviet linguist, held that language is a social class manifestation, and this view was accepted in Soviet linguistic circles until Stalin exploded it with his pronouncement that class languages are only unimportant superstructures upon the edifice of a national language which all social classes hold in common. To this writer's knowledge, Marr's theories have not been revived since Stalin's death.

2. For a detailed discussion of this involved controversy, see Iordan and Orr, *op. cit.,* pp. 112–114, 124, 128, 290, 310, 314, 353.

PROBLEM VI

Classification

IN THE matter of classification of languages, the ancients, being uninterested in "barbarous" tongues, have practically nothing to offer. The very idea of classifying languages, in one fashion or another, does not seem to have arisen until the sixteenth century, and then largely as guesswork based on a few elementary observations, like Sassetti's comment that Sanskrit bore some striking vocabulary resemblances to Italian. Full-scale attempts at classification, but on principles that modern linguistics would consider unscientific, really begin with Bibliander, Gesner, and, particularly, Scaliger.[1] Early classifications, based partly on unhappy etymologies, partly on preconceived theories about the origin of language, are highly unsatisfactory. Leibniz, in the eighteenth century, did a little better; but his Aramaean and Japhetic languages (the latter subdivided into Scythic and Celtic, or what we would call Ural-Altaic and Indo-European; he correctly establishes a separate class for Basque) still constitute a very rudimentary system of classification.

The nineteenth century, with its precise comparative methodology, ultimately offered us the genetic classification in use today. But the problem is far from completely solved.

A genetic classification means that we place under one heading those languages which give indication of stemming from a common ancestor. What is the nature of the indications?

In the field of sounds, it is vain to look for identical or even similar sound patterns between two languages that we suspect are allied. The sound patterns of Italian and French, for instance, or of English and German, do not indicate the similarity that the known history of the languages would lead us to expect. What counts instead is a system of sound correspondences in words that we are reasonably certain are native in the two languages. If an entire series of words not likely to have been borrowed shows that English consistently has *f* where Latin has *p* (*father, foot, for; pater, ped-, per*), the evidence begins to accumulate; it becomes cogent when we discover that practically every sound in one language has a consistent, though not necessarily identical counterpart, in the other. The yardstick is not identity or even similarity of sounds (though these often appear), but consistency in the shift, where it occurs.

In the field of morphology, a basic similarity in grammatical pattern shown by the two languages in their earliest recorded stages supplies very acceptable proof. If we discover that Sanskrit, Greek, Latin, Russian and Anglo-Saxon (not modern English, which has evolved away from its known original pattern) show identical or highly similar grammatical categories, case endings, verb endings, etc., the supposition that they are linked becomes strong. If, on the other hand, there is no resemblance whatsoever in the grammatical pattern of two languages (Latin and Chinese, for instance), the possibility of an original link between them grows remote.

Vocabulary resemblances can be trusted only to a degree. Languages are far too prone to borrow words from one another when they come in contact. The only vocabulary elements we can trust are those where there is no evidence, historical or logical, of borrowing. Usually, but not always, such elements include nouns of family relationship (*father, mother, sister, brother*), numerals, pronouns, a few basic verbs and prepositions.

While the genetic system of affiliation and classification, based on the comparative methodology outlined above, is probably the best at our disposal, it has large gaps. These consist of insufficient recorded material, in the case of many extinct languages, such as Iberian; of failure to decipher the meaning of other extinct languages, like Etruscan; in the case of living langauges, there is the lack of material bearing on their past evolution. (This makes such languages as the native Australian, the African Negro, and particularly the American Indian very difficult to classify.)

The other great system of classification which has received acceptance is the one proposed by H. Steinthal[2] and F. N. Fink.[3] Here the languages are classified according to outward linguistic type, which means, in substance, grammatical structure alone, without reference to sound correspondences or vocabulary. The great divisions here are into isolating languages (making no formal distinction of parts of speech, like Chinese); juxtaposing languages (using classifying prefixes, like Bantu); agglutinative languages (adding independent, fully separable elements to a word root to extend its meaning, like Turkish); polysynthetic or incorporating languages (combining into a single unit the various parts of a sentence, none of which enjoys too much in the way of a separate existence, like Eskimo or Basque); and inflectional or synthetic (using endings or other elements of inflection, which enjoy no separate existence, like Latin or Arabic).

This system of classification is open to historical objections (a language like English, originally inflectional, may in the course of its development go over in part or even entirely to an isolating structure), as well as logical ones (some languages may fit into either of two pigeonholes, depending on which features are viewed as paramount; the differences between agglutinative and inflectional may be of degree rather than kind, or they may have a purely historical explanation).

As matters stand, the question of classification hinges upon that of monogenesis. If we follow the genetic classification, based on a comparative methodology, we run into numerous dead ends, and are left with an amazingly large number of seemingly unrelated families, which might, however, turn out to be related if we had more information. Under these circumstances, it is customary for the geneticists to have recourse, purely for purposes of convenience, to a secondary system of classification, the geographical.

We then have on the one hand a limited number of well-defined language families, concerning the relationship of whose members we have reasonable certainty. This permits us to speak of Indo-European languages, Semitic (and even Semito-Hamitic) languages, Uralic and Altaic languages, Sino-Tibetan languages, Dravidian languages, Malayo-Polynesian languages, even of Bantu and Caucasian languages, all of which display a more or less demonstrable genetic relationship within each group. Then, on the other hand, we have such purely geographic groupings as Sudanese-Guinean (435 languages, tentatively divided up into sixteen major groups, for each of which there is some genetic evidence, but no truly demonstrable relationship among the sixteen groups); American Indian (over 1,200 languages, tentatively distributed among some 125 groups); Australian, Tasmanian and Papuan (about 240 languages, grouping undetermined).[4]

In addition, our genetic system leaves in dispute several possible links, of which the two most important are the link between Japanese and Korean and that between the Uralic and the Altaic tongues. In both cases, there is similarity of grammatical structure, but little that is clearly demonstrable in the way of sound correspondences or vocabulary similarities.

Other problems are posed by the apparent isolation of languages like ancient Etruscan and modern Basque. Can they be linked with a series of vanished "Mediterranean" tongues, and these in turn with the Caucasian family?

Even within groups of which we are as reasonably certain as Indo-European, there appear special problems of affiliation and classification. Was there a period of unity for Italic and Celtic? Are we justified in establishing an Italic classification for Latin, Oscan and Umbrian, or should the latter languages be separately classified, perhaps even linked with primitive Germanic? Did the Indo-European languages spread out from the original parent tongue like branches from the trunk of a tree, or did they proceed like wave rings when one casts a pebble into a pond? (This formed the subject of an interesting controversy between A. Schleicher[5] and J. Schmidt.)[6] Is there anything to the peripheral hypothesis of A. Meillet (since Italo-Celtic at the western end of the Indo-European domain and Indo-Iranian at the eastern end have certain characteristics in common which are not shared with any of the branches in between, they must have broken off from the parent speech earlier than the others)?[7] Was the original Indo-European homeland the Iranian plateau, as the earlier scholars held, or the shores of the Baltic, as would seem indicated by the words for animals, trees, plants and minerals which the Indo-European languages hold in common, since the objects appear largely in that area?

Save in cases where the evidence is clear-cut and overwhelming, it seems as though the basis of the classification depends upon what each individual scholar or school considers to be the most important and relevant features. Is it quite proper to make sound correspondences paramount, as most of the comparativists do,[8] or should we attribute considerable importance to grammatical structure and vocabulary elements, even where the latter do not lend themselves to sound correspondences?

When grammatical structure undergoes a radical change (as in the case of semi-isolating modern English stemming from a highly inflectional Anglo-Saxon, or of modern agglutinative Hindustani stemming from an even more highly inflectional Sanskrit), genetic reasoning would dictate that we keep the language in the classification to which it originally belonged. But structural criteria would favor our shifting the classification. It has been repeatedly pointed out by modern structural linguists that modern spoken French, however much it may have come from an original Latin, today bears strong structural resemblances on the one hand to some of the polysynthetic languages of the American Indians (the unit of understanding in a modern French sentence is normally the entire sentence, or at least the phrase or word group, not the individual word, as evidenced by A. Guérard's transcription of *Je t'offre un bock* as SHTOFŬBOK); on the other, to the African Bantu languages, with their classifying prefixes (*le mur, les murs,* where in speech the distinction between singular and plural is carried by the article, not by the noun ending). Again, when it comes to vocabulary, it is all very well to classify English as genetically Germanic; but more than half its words, even with allowance made for frequency of occurrence, are Greek, Latin and Romance, which leads some people, not linguistically trained but highly educated nevertheless, to reject the straight Germanic classification and claim that English is a blend.

These major and minor controversies on classification may not in the final analysis be too fruitful, but they open up some fascinating vistas. There are many individual ways of classifying languages, depending on the individual viewer and his purpose at the moment. One might, for example, for purposes of practical instruction, establish a classification based on whether a language handles its unstressed vowels clearly or unclearly; on the basis of such a classification, genetically Romance Italian and Spanish and genetically Slavic, Polish, Czech and Serbo-Croatian would fall into a "clear" classification, while genetically Romance Portuguese, Slavic Russian and Germanic English would as obviously fall into an "unclear" class.

Or a classification might be based on syllabic structure. Those tongues which make it a practice to end the syllable in a vowel wherever possible (like Italian, Spanish, Japanese and Indonesian) might be opposed to those that prefer a predominance of consonant endings for the syllable (like English or German).

All this may seem arbitrary, even visionary. Actually, it is frequently done and almost as frequently accepted in reputable circles. Romance linguists have established a classification of east and west Romance languages based on nothing more than whether a given language keeps or drops Latin final -s (to this, progressive voicing of intervocalic consonants is often added, but this theory fails to hold any water).[9] Such a classification disregards a host of other features, in which the geographically contiguous western Romance tongues are opposed to isolated Rumanian.

It is perhaps time to point out to linguists that the scientific attitude, in language classification and elsewhere, calls for an examination and evaluation of *all* the available evidence, not merely of that part of it which happens to suit our thesis at the moment.[10]

NOTES TO PROBLEM VI

1. See Introduction (*History of Linguistics*), n. 5.
2. *Classification der Sprachen,* Berlin, 1850; *Charakteristik der hauptsächlichsten Typen des Sprachbaues,* Berlin, 1860.

3. *Haupttypen des Sprachbaues,* Leipzig, 1910.

4. Gray, *op. cit.,* p. 418.

5. *Beiträge zur vergleichenden Sprachforschung,* 1868.

6. *Die Verwandschaftsverhältnisse der indogermanischen Sprachen,* Weimar, 1872.

7. A. Meillet, *Esquisse d'une histoire de la langue latine,* 2nd ed., p. 285 *f*; and particularly M. Bartoli, whose views on lateral areas, expressed in various of his works, are summarized in Iordan and Orr, *op. cit.,* p. 276, n. 1.

8. Gray, *op. cit.,* pp. 74–83, 301–302.

9. M. Pei, "Intervocalic Occlusives in 'East' and 'West' Romance," *Romanic Review,* XXXIV, 3 (Oct. 1943), pp. 235–247. See also M. Pei, *Reply to R. A. Hall, Jr.'s review of The Italian Language and B. Bloch's review of Languages for War and Peace,* New York, Vanni, 1946.

10. M. Pei, "A New Methodology of Romance Classification," *Word,* V, 2 (Aug. 1949), pp. 135–146.

Advantages and Disadvantages of the Comparative Method

THERE is no question that the comparative methodology inaugurated at the outset of the nineteenth century by Rask, Bopp, Grimm and others laid the foundation for a truly scientific study of language, one that would eliminate guesswork and repress the fanciful hypotheses and etymologies that had previously roamed the field.

But the comparative method posed its own peculiar problems. What forms should be laid down side by side for comparison? Obviously, attested forms, forms that one can trust. In $x + y = z$, at least two of the terms have to be known before we can determine the value of the third term. In like manner, comparativism calls for at least two sure forms from which the hypothetical ancestor can be reconstructed, or for a definite ancestral form plus at least one known descendant to determine what the other descendant may be. Since in the Indo-European field there could be no question of producing an attested parent language, the problem was to find among the descendants usable attested forms from which the parent tongue could be reconstructed. The value of inscriptional and documentary evidence from the older attested languages thus became paramount.

There was only one thing that might possibly be wrong with these attested forms. They were all in writing, since the native speakers were all dead, and there had been no phonograph or tape recordings at the time when these ancient languages were spoken. Could it possibly be that some of these written forms, found in inscriptions, papyri and parchments, might diverge from the spoken forms of the period from which they were supposed to issue?

This problem was not even considered at the outset. It was implicitly taken for granted by all early comparativists that the written evidence was one hundred per cent valid. It still does not occur today to scholars working in Hittite, Tokharian, Sanskrit, early Greek, Gothic, or Church Slavonic to doubt the validity of their written evidence, on grounds of possible divergence from the spoken tongues. The doubts arose only when Friedrich Diez undertook to apply the comparative method to the Romance languages.[1]

Here the common ancestor was fully known. Latin had enjoyed continuous existence, in one form or another, from about 500 A.D. to the present. But Latin, in the course of well over ten centuries during which it had been a spoken popular tongue, had undergone numerous changes. Did the Romance forms that were under comparison stem from Classical Latin, archaic Latin, or late Latin? In many cases, the comparison did not jibe with any of the attested forms. What to do?

Two courses were possible. One was to intensify research in the abundant documentation offered by Latin itself, at all historical periods, in the hope of finding forms that would square better with the comparison. The other could be described as the course of least resistance: where a Romance comparison did not coincide with attested documentary or inscriptional Latin forms, throw out the Latin forms as irrelevant from the standpoint of the spoken language, and use the comparative method in the same fashion in which it was used by the Indo-Europeanists.

The latter had been enjoying themselves playing a fascinating game, that of hypothetical reconstruction. Placing side by side all their attested forms, from Sanskrit, Latin, Greek, Gothic, Slavic, Armenian, Old Irish, they would then proceed to rebuild the Indo-European ancestor form. The initiator of this game was A. Schleicher, who in his *Compendium der vergleichenden Grammatik der indogermanischen Sprachen* (Weimar, 1876) had proceeded to "reconstruct" the Indo-European parent tongue from a comparison of the attested tongues, in the same fashion in which paleontologists reconstruct a hypothetical parent species of animal from a comparison of the traits of the available descendants. Schleicher had even invented the use of the asterisk, or starred form, whereby the reader is given to understand that the form cited is not attested, but reconstructed. He had even composed an Indo-European fable entitled *Avis akvāsas ka,* "The sheep and the horse." (The Latin equivalent, Latin being one of the languages that enter into the comparison at the base of the reconstruction, is *ovis equusque.*)

Indo-Europeanists are at great pains to tell us that these reconstructed Indo-European forms are only hypothetical, that they must not be taken too seriously, that Indo-European itself may never have had any real existence. Actually, they believe implicitly in their reconstructed creations, and base all their calculations upon them, employing an interesting variety of circular reasoning in their deductions. (For instance, a certain Greek form does not jibe with the hypothetical Indo-European form arrived at by comparing forms in Sanskrit, Latin, Gothic and a few other early languages; therefore, the Greek form in question cannot possibly be linked with the others, despite similarities in form and meaning.) As recently as 1959, our most authoritative work in the field of Indo-European etymologies (J. Pokorny's *Indogermanisches etymologisches Wörterbuch,* Bern, 1951–1959) is based squarely upon reconstructed Indo-European roots, which are only occasionally and hesitatingly presented in two or more variant forms to account for the vagaries of the daughter tongues.

Do these somewhat questionable procedures invalidate the comparative method? Not at all. In fact, I am a little contemptuous of the hedgings with which many Indo-Europeanists surround their references to their parent tongue. Granted the existence of an entire series of Indo-European languages, what is wrong with the idea of a parent tongue, spoken, very probably, by a homogeneous group of speakers whose racial characteristics may or may not have coincided with those that certain anthropologists attribute to what they call the "Nordic" race? There has been enough mingling of both races and languages since proto-Indo-European times to do away with any racialistic conclusion of the Nazi-inspired variety. It is enough to state that the reconstructions are in part hypothetical and doubtful, and that Indo-European and Indo-European languages are not meant to convey any racial connotations. It is not necessary to add, hypocritically, that speakers of Indo-European may never have existed, and that all we are trying to do is to establish a system of sound correspondences among the attested members of the family, something that none of us really believes.

The Indo-European scholar reconstructs his hypothetical Indo-European because there is nothing else he can really do if he wants to account for his sound correspondences. In like manner, the American Indian specialist has no recourse but to procure one or more native speakers, and figure out the structure of the language from the translation of the phrases and sentences he gives them, as will be brought out later.

But these methodologies are not merely unnecessary, but wasteful and misleading when there is a wealth of real documentary evidence, as is the case with Romance development. In the specific instance of the reconstruction of a hypothetical Vulgar Latin, when we have all the Vulgar Latin material in the world at our disposal, and our only problem is to search through it to find what we want, there may be sheer intellectual laziness.

The basic methodological error of Romance specialists who place their reliance upon comparativism rather than documentary research has often been pointed out.[2] Two points, however, are just as often offered in rebuttal. The first is that in the case of certain languages, Latin among them, there is a crystallization of the written language, which, at a certain point, ceases to follow the evolution of the spoken tongue and becomes, to all intents and purposes, a dead language, from which nothing can be gathered save traditional features used by scribes for centuries after the spoken tongue had departed from them. The second is that nowhere, and at no historical period, does the written language ever truly reflect the spoken tongue, particularly that of the masses.

It is interesting in connection with the first point that no member of this school of thought has ever coincided with another in his estimation of the point where the process of divergence began. Granting, as one undoubtedly must, though with qualifications that will appear below, that there exists at all times a natural, inherent divergence between a spoken language and its written counterpart, at what point did this divergence assume such an aspect of artificiality that one would have to describe the two languages, spoken and written, as separate and mutually unintelligible? Answers range all the way from the early days of the Republic to the sixth, seventh, and even eighth century A.D.[3]

When these answers are placed too early in history, they tend to merge with the second disclaimer, which is to the effect that no written language ever reflects its spoken counterpart.[4] If we accept this thesis, we may as well say good-by to our comparative method, since all early attested forms (in Sanskrit, Greek, Gothic, or what have you, as well as in Latin), being written, become valueless.

Actually, what is needed here again is the exercise of proper research and ingenuity to sift out of a written inscription or text what is artificial and what is a true reflection of speech. But this calls for real hard work, and it is so much easier to throw up our hands and say it can't be done.

A moment's reflection will show us that no written language in general use that is based upon any kind of phonetic notation is utterly divorced from its spoken counterpart. The spoken Arabic vernaculars may diverge to a greater or lesser degree from Classical Arabic, but they are nevertheless based on it and related to it, and Classical Arabic itself is very much a spoken language for international intercourse among the Arab lands, and even for cultural internal use. The written English language today has its connections with both British and American vernaculars, however dialectal or slangy.

We can go along with the theory that the spoken Latin of the circus and the provinces diverged from the language of the loftiest Latin poets to the same extent that the language of the streets in London, New York, Atlanta or Manchester diverges from the tongue of Emily Dickinson and Robert Browning. But the Latin documentary material at our disposal is far from limited to Virgil and Horace. We have Plautus, tombstone inscriptions, Pompeiian graffiti, Petronius, private deeds of sale, veterinary treatises, religious works for popular consumption, and a host of other things. Much of this material has been only superficially examined, usually in search of some specific feature.

It is at present a favorite sport among some linguists to reconstruct the sound scheme of spoken Latin, or Primitive Romance, or Old French, from a mass of indications based upon the present-day Romance dialects, with materials drawn from the linguistic atlases, which are altogether modern.[5] This sort of comparative evidence is preferred to documentary proof from the period which it is proposed to describe. But numerous obscure historical factors may have intervened between the ancient tongue and the present-day dialects.

Comparison is not only useful, but necessary. Reconstruction is desirable only in certain cases. Granting that documentary evidence may at times be misleading, to ignore it in historical linguistics is tantamount to rejecting the value of all documentation in historical research.

NOTES TO PROBLEM VII

1. *Grammatik der romanischen Sprachen*, 1836–1844.

2. See Iordan and Orr, *op. cit.*, pp. 4–5; H. Schuchardt, *Brevier*, Halle, 1928, p. 204 f.; A. Meillet, in *Bulletin de la Société de Linguistique de Paris*, XXI (1917–1919), p. 230.

3. To cite only two extremes, see F. Mohl, *Introduction à la chronologie du latin vulgaire*, Paris, 1927, and H. F. Muller, "Chronology of Vulgar Latin," in *Zeitschrift für romanische Philologie*, Beiheft 78, 1929; "When Did Latin Cease to Be a Spoken Language in France?" *Romanic Review*, XII (1921), pp. 318–339.

4. E. Pulgram, "Spoken and Written Latin," *Language*, 26.4.458–466 (Oct.-Dec. 1950).

5. R. A. Hall, Jr., "Old French Phonemes and Orthography," *Studies in Romance Philology*, XLIII (1946), pp. 575–585; "The Reconstruction of Proto-Romance," *Language*, 26.1 (1950), pp. 6–27.

Descriptivism vs. Historicism

HISTORICAL, or diachronic linguistics deals with the study of language as it unfolds across time. Descriptive, or synchronic linguistics deals with the study of language as it appears at a given point in time, which is usually the present; but interesting attempts have been made in recent times to reconstruct the synchronic picture of a language at one point or another in the past.[1]

Antiquity and the Middle Ages present unscientific attempts at both types of linguistics. In fact, the attempts go back so far that we are left in some doubt as to which came first. Biblical and Greek discussions on the origin of language display undoubted historical features, however erroneous; while any attempt to explain one language in terms of another, such as must have attended the training of Akkadian and Egyptian diplomatic interpreters, must of necessity involve descriptive features, however rudimentary.

We have already seen that ancient and medieval attempts at historical linguistics were based on unsound premises. Greater luck seems to have attended descriptivism in those periods, even though the results would not have satisfied a modern linguist. Panini's grammar of Sanskrit, the numerous grammars of Greek and Latin produced in antiquity, medieval phrase books like the

Glosses of Reichenau and Kassel, Aelfric's eleventh-century Latin-Saxon grammar, were all descriptive in nature, though for the most part fraught with a prescriptive element which modern linguistics would reject. The numerous grammars of various tongues, old and newly discovered, that range from the fifteenth century to our own times, all have descriptive purposes. The historical approach, on the other hand, does not assume truly scientific aspects until the birth of comparativism, in the early nineteenth century.

The inception of the comparative method, which is basically historical, also marked its almost absolute predominance in the field of linguistics. While diachronic research became a truly scholarly topic, reserved only for superior minds, descriptivism continued to be, throughout the nineteenth century, what it had been in earlier centuries—a practical, utilitarian subject, exemplified by the writing of grammars for purposes of learning foreign tongues or of telling you how properly to use your own.

Modern languages and dialects were largely overlooked in the process of historical reconstruction of Indo-European, Vulgar Latin, and other parent languages. For this, there was an obvious reason: the comparative method demanded that the earliest, not the latest forms of a language be ranged side by side for comparison. The more one was forced to come down into modern times for his language samples, the more the situation was complicated and confused by late historical developments, many of them obscure. For nineteenth-century purposes, Homeric Greek was far better than Byzantine or modern Greek, Sanskrit than Hindustani, Dante's Italian more valuable than Manzoni's.

It is true that the same Schleicher who attempted the full-scale reconstruction of Indo-European pointed to the importance of living Lithuanian as a language that by reason of its unchanged, archaic structure offered great reconstructive possibilities; but his purpose was clearly historical, and his living language just as clearly archaic and unchanged. On the other hand, von Humboldt, in his *Ueber die Kawisprache* (1836–1837), began to present a classification of the non-Indo-European languages, and many of these could be offered only in their modern form.

The true change in point of view, and the presentation of descriptive linguistics as an equal partner with historical linguistics, came with De Saussure, whose *Cours de linguistique générale,* published in 1916 after his death, carefully outlined the boundaries and functions of the two kindred branches. De Saussure's views of descriptive linguistics as equally important with historical linguistics received a powerful fillip from the appearance of linguistic geography and the earliest of the linguistic atlases (J. Gilliéron and E. Edmont's *Atlas linguistique de la France,* 1902–1910). This relatively young branch of linguistics (it had been heralded by Martin Sarmiento in his *Dicionário geral das linguas románicas,*[2] but nothing had come of it at the time) deals exclusively with present-day linguistic realities. Its original purpose was to serve as an auxiliary in the dialect studies which had become the vogue, largely as a result of the attempt on the part of the Neolinguists to disprove the cogency of the sound laws of the Neogrammarians.

But now that it had been established that it was nonsense, on a basis of objective reality, to speak of a French or Italian "language" when the linguistic atlas showed that there were as many separate French or Italian "languages" as there were French or Italian localities, the spotlight began to shift from the demonstration to the method. Disregarding both national unities and national standard languages, eschewing all documents of the ancient and modern written tongues, and even of written dialects, sending out field workers to extract from local inhabitants (the more illiterate the better) the local speech forms, and recording these in phonetic transcriptions—such was the basis of the new science of linguistic geography.[3] Obviously, the finished product of an investigation of this kind would cast only an indirect and dubious light upon the historical evolution of the language, but it would yield an absolute, incontrovertible picture of the present-day stage, based on purely descriptive criteria which would contain no element of either historicism or prescriptivism. The true linguistic state of a nation, region or group would stand forth in all its stark nakedness, utterly divorced from both national standards and normative prescriptions as to what people ought to speak.

Both De Saussure's great principle of general linguistics and the methodology of linguistic geography were enthusiastically embraced by those linguists who had been devoting their efforts to investigating the little known, obscure, politically unimportant, unwritten and unrecorded languages. Relieved of the necessity of delving into hypothetical Indo-European ablauts and pharyngeals, consonant and vowel shifts often based on insufficient documentary evidence, illegible inscriptions and musty medieval parchments, the new descriptivist generation plunged with zest into the work of recording from real, living native speakers the speech forms actually in use.

In the United States in particular, several new-school linguists with anthropological leanings had been busily recording the speech forms of near-extinct American Indian groups. F. Boas, with his *Handbook of American Indian Languages,* 1907, was one of the earliest contributors to this field. Other pioneers were E. Sapir (*Language,* 1921) and L. Bloomfield (*Language,* 1933). Their early work was viewed as scientifically interesting, but not particularly important, since they were dealing with languages which had neither political prominence nor a cultural history. The big break for the anthropological linguists and their methodology came with the Second World War, when many languages hitherto neglected suddenly acquired strategic relevance in connection with various campaigns undertaken by the U.S. Armed Forces.

One justification that had been offered for the research methodology of the new school of anthropological linguistics (basically an extension of the methodology followed in the compilation of linguistic atlases) was that in the case of the languages in which they were working no other methodology was possible. American Indian languages have no known history, no written documents or written form (with the possible, slightly doubtful exception of the tongues of the Mayas and Aztecs), nothing save surviving native speakers. Therefore, it was highly legitimate to concentrate on the native speakers and extract from them the necessary information on the basis of which a grammar and vocabulary could be based.

But the anthropological linguists boldly rejected this justification, based themselves on the Saussurian definition of general, descriptive linguistics, and offered the thesis that theirs was by far the best, not to say the only, methodology for the study and description of living languages. (Some of them have recently gone even farther, and attempted to prove that it is the best, not to say the only, methodology for the study and description of dead languages as well.)[4] These assertions were coupled with slashing attacks on old methods of language teaching and language learning, but the nature of these attacks will be described later.

The new-school writers, while extremely vociferous in their condemnation of old-style grammars and prescriptive manuals, are generally silent for what concerns the scientific merits or importance of the historical branch of linguistics based on documented forms, save where they indicate, by their attempts at replacing its traditional methodology, that they hold it in contempt. Their real concern is with the modern spoken tongues, dialects and idiolects.

This means that their approach (and, indeed, the entire descriptive approach and methodology) has an intensely practical aspect, transcending mere academic research and reaching down into the field of pedagogy and the philosophy of language learning.

It is the contention of the descriptivists (and particularly of the American descriptivists) that the only form of language worthy of the name is the spoken variety, and that our view of this should be based squarely upon what people actually speak, not upon the normative prescriptions contained in traditional grammars. Practical applications of this proposition are that the spoken language should be learned first, with writing brought in later, if at all; that the best form of language to learn is that practiced by the majority of the speakers, even if condemned by normative grammars; that the assimilation of native-speaker sounds is of paramount importance, transcending either grammatical structure or vocabulary acquisition (but this stand has been somewhat modified in recent times); that the comparison of one language with another is harmful in the language-learning process, though not, presumably, in the historical study of languages, if anyone still cares to go into that antiquated pursuit (here again, there have been some rather spectacular recent shifts).[5]

All this is a little breath-taking, but only because of the fact that the American school has mixed up two issues that are basically unrelated: the methodology of linguistic research and the methodology of language learning.

For what concerns the latter, once we make allowance for some of the bombastic exaggerations voiced by some members of the group, the new school has a good deal in its favor. For the purpose of learning to speak and understand a language for conversational use, there is no denying that stress, particularly at the outset, should be placed on the spoken rather than on the written language; on the general colloquial standard rather than on the rarefied tongue of antiquated literature (but not on substandard or dialect forms, save for specific purposes) ; on the sounds of the spoken language (but only in close conjunction with basic grammatical patterns and a basic practical vocabulary) ; and with general avoidance of that so-called "cultural" material which, whether it be philological, literary, folkloristic or anything else, distracts the learner from his basic purpose, which is to learn the language, not to learn about the language.

In connection with the purely scientific study of language and languages, the basic philosophy of descriptivism, as outlined by De Saussure, may be accepted in its entirety. Its present-day extensions are something else. It should not be allowed to crowd the historical, comparative approach out of the picture, as it too often tends to do. Its methodology, in general, is not applicable to historical problems, which should be solved on the basis of available evidence, not of descriptivistic theory. Descriptivists should realize, once and for all, that a methodology that is the only one applicable in the case of Kwakiutl or Choctaw need not be the only one applicable to French or German.

Recent extensions of descriptivism are many, varied, and, in some aspects, laudable. To mention only two, we have the structuralism propounded by the Prague School and outlined in its possible historical applications in A. Martinet's *Economie des changements phonétiques* (1955) ; in oversimplified form, this theory is to the effect that language changes do not occur at random, or as a series of individual and unrelated phenomena, but in accordance with a pattern involving an entire series of related sounds (for instance, a language that has in its phonemic pattern k, t, p, and g, d, but not b, will tend to make its pattern symmetrical by either bringing in b or dropping p) ; and the

Glossematics of L. Hjelmslev (an attempt to present language and language change as a series of mathematical formulas). These and other theories are still in the controversial stage; but they illustrate the tendency of the descriptive school to invade the historical field.

NOTES TO PROBLEM VIII

1. See Problem VII, n. 5.

2. Despite all attempts made, it has been impossible for us to locate a copy of this work, either in American or in Portuguese libraries. Its existence and the material it contains are therefore in the nature of hearsay evidence.

3. S. Pop, *La Dialectologie,* Louvain, 1950, is the fundamental work on this methodology.

4. H. M. Hoenigswald, *Language Change and Linguistic Reconstruction,* Chicago, 1960; and see my review, *Modern Language Journal,* XLIV, 7 (Nov. 1960), pp. 335–336.

5. Compare, for example, the very recent book by R. Lado, *Linguistics Across Cultures* (with foreword by C. Fries), University of Michigan Press, Ann Arbor, 1957 (*How to Compare: two Sound Systems; two Grammatical Structures; two Vocabulary Systems; two Writing Systems; two Cultures*) with earlier directives, as voiced by L. Bloomfield, *Outline Guide for the Practical Study of Foreign Languages,* Linguistic Society of America, Baltimore, 1942, pp. 1–2, to the effect that "to get an easy command of a foreign language one must learn to ignore the features of any and all other languages, especially of one's own."

Linguistics: A Physical or a Social Science?

THIS is a purely modern problem, since it obviously could not arise, at least consciously, until the physical and social sciences (particularly the former) had come into being.

The Greeks, in their philosophical discussions, gave evidence of a point of view which, translated into modern terms, would have placed them among the supporters of the social science view of language. Aristotle's "social contract" view is particularly indicative of this. Perhaps, by stretching a point, we could include the believers in "nature" among those who today would view language as a physical manifestation. But all this is rather far-fetched.

The first real hint that linguistics should be treated as a physical science comes with the mechanistic position of the Neogrammarians and the creation of the *Lautgesetz*. The Neolinguist reaction to this stand is largely a sociological one, language being made to depend upon the individual and the group, both of which are subject to all sorts of sociological influences.

Both sides of the argument have their justification. For the view of language as a physical science topic, it may be alleged that language consists basically of sounds, which are produced and received by physiological organs and transmitted by sound waves. This means that language, at least for its phonological division, can be described in terms of physiology and physics. Even the psychological aspects of language can be physically classified if we interpret psychology as a part of neurology and therefore of physiology. The fact that the full psychological process has not yet been fully described in terms of the physical nervous system does not mean that it may not be so described at some future date. Important research is being carried on in this field at the present time, and more and more instances are coming to light of certain speech activities that are definitely linked with certain areas of the physical brain, accounting for such phenomena as aphasia.

It is equally idle to deny the link between language and the social sciences. Language is a phenomenon that normally goes on in a social environment. It has for its purpose communication, which is the transfer of meaning, almost invariably for a social purpose (in the narrow sense that it involves more than one individual). The influences exerted upon language by all sorts of sociological factors (religion, politics, economics, war, etc.) are too well known to demand repetition. The sociological aspect of language may even be extended to include literature, poetry, and other cultural manifestations of language. It may be true that a literary writer may be primarily concerned with self-expression for his own personal esthetic satisfaction, but rare indeed is the author who does not hope and expect to be read, and to exert some sort of influence upon the minds of others.

Hence the discussion as to whether language should be viewed primarily as a physical or a sociological phenomenon is largely meaningless. It is both. It is up to the individual scholar whether he prefers to concentrate his attention and efforts upon one or another aspect of language, but both aspects are there, in their infinite ramifications. At the most, the choice between putting language among the humanities, the social sciences or the physical sciences may interest educational administrators, for purely administrative purposes.

There are, however, several related issues which lend themselves to discussion. There is, for example, the question, brought into focus by the Soviet language controversy, whether language is primarily a class manifestation or the property of the community at large. Stalin rather brusquely settled the issue, as far as the Soviet Union was concerned, by pronouncing against N. Y. Marr's view of language as a class phenomenon and stating that the Russian tongue of the aristocracy was basically the same as that of the masses. But his unilateral decision need not bind us, or keep us from examining the question further.

It is a well-known fact that language is socially stratified. In Britain there has recently been talk, on the amateur level, of U vs. non-U language; certain usages which are restricted to the upper classes and do not extend to the lower, and other usages of the lower classes which people reared in the Eton-Harrow tradition would not dream of using.

There are plenty of languages where the social or class stratification runs deeper. Javanese assumes a threefold form, Ngoko for the common people, Krama for the aristocracy, and Madya for interchange between the two. Some of the ancient plays of India show the more aristocratic characters using Sanskrit, the lower ones indulging in the Prakrits. In the view of some linguists, Latin was so heavily stratified that the members of the aristocracy could barely achieve understanding with the gladiators and the slaves, though of this there is no demonstrable evidence. Something similar is supposed to happen in American English; but here the evidence seems to point to local rather than class differences as the cause of misunderstanding.

If we are dealing with a single language or dialect, and not with different languages or different local dialects, the social stratification of language seems to proceed in accordance with a fairly definite formula. Of the four divisions of language, phonology (or sounds), morphology (or grammatical forms), syntax (or word arrangement) and vocabulary (or words), the first two seem to be largely common property for all social classes, while the last two are the ones in which big divergences develop and become noticeable.

In a language community, no matter how socially stratified, the pattern of sounds (or phonemes, which are sounds that are distinctively significant to the speakers) is basically the same for all classes. There may be a few minor differences (the lower-class New Yorker may use *dese* and *goil* for the upper-class New Yorker's *these* and *girl*), but they are seldom such as to preclude understanding, partly because each class is thoroughly familiar, from long association, with the other class's sound shifts, partly because the shifts are seldom drastic, as they often are in the case of local dialects.

Basic morphological forms seldom show any pronounced difference from class to class. Whether a speaker of American English is cultured or uncultured, he will generally form his noun plurals and third person singulars of verbs with -*s*, make the generally accepted shifts in past and participial forms, use uninflected adjectives. Here again we may get an occasional class deviation, like "I seen him" for "I saw him"; but again, these will be few, and not of such a nature as to preclude mutual understanding.

When we come to word arrangement, the basic syntactical patterns are fairly universal (subject-verb-object; adjective before the noun). But the upper-class speaker may complicate his basic pattern with numerous subsidiary devices, such as subordinate clauses, which the lower-class speaker will avoid, using brief, choppy sentences. But here we must make a distinction between what happens in writing, or in exalted speech, and what takes place in ordinary conversational exchange. Interesting wire-tapping experiments designed to trap upper-class speakers into revealing their ordinary colloquial patterns have brought to light surprising similarities to the syntax of the lower classes.

The real diversity occurs in vocabulary, where both range and choice vary enormously, not merely from class to class, but from calling to calling. Here each class has its own jargon, its own sets of special words which may easily be unintelligible to nonmembers. The layman's lack of understanding when two physicians are discussing his symptoms and therapy is perhaps extreme, but it is characteristic. Yet no matter what special sets of words come into play, the basic vocabulary is always the same for the entire speech community. Words like *the, and, of, this, who, bread, street, go, walk, come,* are in the common domain.

Stalin, the layman in the field of linguistics, won an easy victory over Marr, the professional, because he recognized the fundamental fact that so-called class languages are nothing but unimportant superstructures on the basic edifice of language.

But while the class element plays a relatively unimportant role in language taken at any given stage, it seems to exert a much more profound influence on the rate and speed of language change. Here it is the factor of prestige that comes into play. The upper classes tend to be more conservative, the lower more revolutionary in their language habits. At historical periods when the upper classes hold decided sway over the social structure, the rate of language change is perceptibly slowed. When the prestige of the upper classes wanes, innovations become more numerous and profound. The first phenomenon occurred during the Classical period of Latin, when social stability and upper-class dominance coincided with the spreading of a fairly uniform Latin over wide territorial areas, and with its long conservation. The second phenomenon occurred when the prestige of the Roman upper classes waned, as a result of the spreading of Christianity, which was at first distinctly a lower-class movement. The process of imitation of the persons admired was the same. But now the persons admired were no longer the members of the senatorial and equestrian classes, but the lowly fishermen and slaves who were spreading Christ's Gospel.

Is language change a mass phenomenon, or is it due to individual innovations? The writers of the Romantic period believed in mass change, and this may have influenced the mechanists in their formulation of the sound laws. It is perfectly true that the bulk of language innovations is of anonymous origin. But anonymous does not coincide with mass or group. The mere fact that we do not know who started a particular innovation does not mean that it was not an individual, endowed with prestige and deemed worthy of imitation in his own limited circle, with the imitation later spreading to other circles.

There is, however, another possibility at the root of language change, and that is imperfect production and imperfect reception of sounds. This brings us squarely back to the mechanistic, physical science view of language and language change. A speaker pronounces imperfectly, sometimes by reason of a speech impediment, more often because he wants to achieve greater rapidity and emphasis of speech; or a hearer misinterprets the sound he hears, and reproduces it in modified form. All this occurs in accordance with mechanical, physiological or acoustic factors.

But even if this view is accepted, the fact remains that the imperfect imitator, or the imitator of an imperfection, must himself have imitators for the innovation to spread. The spreading of the innovation, whatever be its original causes, must perforce take place by a sociological rather than a mechanical process.

At any rate, the theory of economy of effort, or basic laziness on the part of the speakers, does not coincide with the facts. If this theory were correct, all younger languages would be easier to pronounce than the tongues from which they sprang. Such is far from the case, as one can see from a comparison of the sound schemes of, say, Latin and French, particularly Old French. The processes of language change are due to factors far more complex than a mere desire on the part of the speakers to make things easier for themselves.[1]

NOTE TO PROBLEM IX

1. For the specific causes of language change in the transition from Latin to Romance, see M. Pei, *The Italian Language,* New York, 1941, pp. 16–24. It is a myth among many linguists, both historical and descriptive, that language change is due to basic laziness of the speakers, and their desire to reduce the effort of speaking. If this were true, all languages would be reduced to mere vowel sequences, since vowel sounds are the ones requiring least effort of the vocal apparatus. Instead, we see everywhere widespread syncopation of unstressed vowels, with consequent formation of consonant clusters that call for considerable expenditure of effort on the speaker's part. All observation, both historical and descriptive, indicates that the basic psychological feature behind language change is not a desire for ease on the speakers' part, but a desire for emphasis coupled with speed. The average speaker wants to be emphatic in what he says, because he normally considers his statement to be of paramount importance. At the same time, he wants to speak fast, partly so as not to give his listener a chance to break in, partly because he wants to crowd more of his all-important utterances into a shorter period of time, so as to save time for more all-important utterances. All this, of course, takes place in normal, unrestrained, uninhibited conversational interchange, which constitutes at least 90 per cent of all speech activity. Deliberate, measured utterance is characteristic of orators and after-dinner speakers, who normally have to fear no interruption and are not pressed for time, even if their audiences are.

Esthetics in Language

IN A purely scientific sense, this problem is nonexistent. Language and languages have their own objective reality. Esthetically pleasing or not, they are what they are, and nothing more need be said.

Yet it is doubtful if any topic connected with language has ever aroused greater or more bitter controversy. The controversy has not one, but many facets.

Is language itself beautiful? Should it be beautiful? Is one language more esthetically pleasing than another? Is one dialectal or class form of a language superior to another? Is it possible to use language in such a way as to arouse an esthetic impression? If so, should the esthetic features of language take precedence over its communicative aspect? Are there spiritual forces in language, which rule and guide its creation and development? Is the spirit of a language displayed by its choice of words and constructions, by its imagery? Is there a poetic as well as a scientific aspect to the pursuits of the linguist? Is there such a thing as taste in language?

Each and every one of these questions can be answered, but only by a subjective, personal judgment. Answers are implicit in most of the statements that have been made on the subject of language throughout recorded history.

At all times and in all places, speakers of a given language have considered and pronounced that language beautiful. It is their own possession, and shares the personal connotations that surround the concepts of home, family, native land, religion, and a host of other components of what the anthropologists call "culture." It is only exceptionally that a man will condemn his place of birth, the members of his household, his close friends, the faith of his fathers. Language is fraught with the same associations, strengthened, perhaps, by the feature of unconsciousness in the use of language.

Extolling one's own tongue, condemning other tongues is something so frequently, and so irrationally, exemplified throughout history that volumes could be written on the subject. The ancient Greeks considered their own language beautiful, but non-Greeks were "barbarians," or "stammerers." The Middle Ages present occasional examples of the ridiculing of other tongues, as when the Italian monks poke fun at the uncouth speech of their Gothic brethren, or Olivier Basselin at the language of the English invaders. Such epithets as *Nemtsy* ("dumb"), conferred by the speakers of Slavic upon their German neighbors, are there to indicate that the attitude is widespread. There are numerous panegyrics, defenses and illustrations of the various vernaculars, composed by their own speakers, which come down to our own times.[1] Seldom enough do we get a pronouncement from a speaker of one language on behalf of another tongue, as when Brunetto Latini praises French, or Jakob Grimm and Jespersen praise English. But even this praise is often mingled with utilitarian rather than esthetic considerations, as when a Norwegian thirteenth-century writer advocates learning all languages, "but above all Latin and French, because they are the most widely used."[2] The topic of the esthetic superiority of one language over another may therefore be dismissed as a subject of objective discussion, or, at the most, referred to individual taste, like the preference for French over Chinese cooking.

Even in those functions where an esthetic quality seems to come to the fore (the sounds of a language, or the way in which they are arranged), the judgment is in part subjective, in part utilitarian. One could argue, for instance, that the sound scheme of Italian is more musical than that of English, but that would refer us to the purpose for which the language is used, as well as to our individual sound-scheme preferences, which are necessarily built up on familiarity and habit.

This does not at all mean that we should have no esthetic preferences in language and languages, but merely that we should label them for what they are: esthetic and subjective, not scientific, objective judgments.

With dialectal and class variants of the same language, something similar occurs. Standard versions of a given language, where they exist, seldom arose out of esthetic considerations. They were for the most part dictated by political and military factors. Then, as the other local speech forms sank in prestige, they were deemed esthetically inferior and unworthy of use for higher literary purposes. Since to him who has shall be given, attention and care and esthetic embellishments were lavished upon the official tongues, while the dialects were neglected and left to their own devices.

At the same time, the condemnation of dialectal forms is something so widespread in both time and space as to be almost universal. It ranges all the way from slurring Classical Latin references to the *subrusticus* to Manzoni's disclaimer of his own language as inferior because it was not learned on the banks of the Arno. In between, we have such medieval samples as the one furnished in 1173 by Garnier de Pont-Saint-Maxence, who describes the language in which he depicts the murder of Thomas à Becket as "good, because I was born in the Ile-de-France," Conon of Bethune's bitter complaint, in 1182, of the ridicule cast upon his Artois accent, and Chaucer's prioress whose French was not that of Paris, but that of Stratford. Apologizing for one's dialect is still a favorite pastime, save perhaps in America, where the doctrine of equalitarianism has been extended to the language field.

The use of language to create an esthetic impression is something that concerns the field of literature and style. Yet literature and style, which are primarily esthetic, have to make use of language as their vehicle. But language exists also, and primarily, as a vehicle of ordinary communication shorn of all esthetic pretensions. It is here that an extremist of the mentalistic school, like B. Croce, clashes with the linguists. He maintains that language is primarily and universally a mode of self-expression, an instrument of creation, a result of intuition, which must find expression.[3]

The views of Croce, his precursors, Vico and Herder, and his followers, particularly Vossler, have aroused a great deal of controversy, which is largely needless. Croce, as a philosopher, is describing the psychological process which gives rise to the form of expression, while his critics are concerned with the form of expression itself.

What is distressing in the views of many of Croce's critics is their denial of all spiritual forces which guide the creation and development of language. To regard language creation and language change as a purely mechanical process is tantamount to denying the principle of cause and effect.

An example of this type of thinking appears in B. Bloch and G. L. Trager's *Outline of Linguistic Analysis* (pp. 8–9): "In terms of linguistic science, the only answer to the question Why? is a historical statement. Why do we call an animal of the species *Equus caballus* a horse?—because that is what our parents called it, and their English-speaking ancestors before them for over a thousand years. . . . Attempts to answer the question Why? in other ways—by appeals to psychology, philosophy, or abstract logic—may seem esthetically more satisfying, but are never anything better than guesses, unprovable and fruitless."[4]

The point of view described above is perhaps a reaction to earlier, fanciful interpretations of linguistic phenomena. But there are two things wrong with it: first, it cuts the heart out of linguistics, and makes it truly dry as dust; second, and more important, it shuts out the link between language and the conditions and vicissitudes of the speakers.

Is it logical to suppose that there were no causes for the visible effects? If this were so, why did a language like Latin develop not uniformly, into a single modern Romance, but in a multiplicity of divergent forms? Did not each variety of Romance develop separately in accordance with its own previous or subsequent historical conditions? Precisely what is wrong with endeavoring to trace the possible connection between those historical conditions and the language changes that occurred at the same time, provided a scientific, objective methodology is followed, and conclusions are presented as tentative, not as mathematically proved? Circumstantial evidence, if sufficiently cogent, is acceptable even in a court of law.

To take a single example from the field of Romance development: it is fashionable in certain circles to deny any validity to the theory that the progressive vulgarization of Latin and the consequent evolution of Latin into Romance was aided and speeded by the new spirit of Christianization that swept the Roman Empire in the centuries immediately preceding its fall.[5] Instead, the process is attributed to a variety of mechanical and semi-mechanical factors (East-West roads, Germanic invasions, etc.).[6]

Yet all one has to do is to glance at the one division of language, vocabulary, in which the evidence is not circumstantial, but direct. Here we are faced with a giant expansion of the re-

ligious vocabulary of Latin, spilling over into all sorts of other
fields of activity, with the wholesale importation of religious words
not only from the New Testament, but even from the older
Hebrew and Aramaic. Yet we are asked to believe that a purely
spiritual phenomenon, the fervor of conversion to a new faith of
hope, which had such an influence upon the lexicon, exerted little
or no influence upon the other divisions of language, the sounds,
the grammatical forms, the syntactic arrangements.

Again, we look at the early samples of the new Romance languages, and we find them replete with learned and semi-learned
words pertaining to the vocabulary of religion. Are these words
truly as "learned" as some people think? Were they used only by
the monks and clerics? It is quite obvious, from the type of documents in which they appear, and their survival into the present,
that they are meant for general consumption, and are part and
parcel of the great medieval process of building up religious faith
in the masses. If so, were these so-called learned words not part
of the word stock of those masses, in the very forms in which they
appear, which is normally a highly conservative form? Therefore
did not the spiritual process lead to the freezing, so to speak, of a
large segment of the vocabulary, and to its escape from the iron-
bound "laws" of phonological evolution?

These are the questions that are ignored by those linguists who
hold that their task consists merely of cataloguing and labeling
forms without regard for causes. To deny the pressure of spiritual
influence on language is indicative of the same warped mentality
that has led to the doctrine of economic determinism in history
and to the Marxist view that the universe is all matter and no
spirit. But even the economic determinists and the Marxists admit
the principle of cause and effect, which the mechanistic linguists
deny or affect to ignore.

The linguist ought not to exclude from his study of language any of the factors that may shed light upon it. In so doing, he will not merely be more scientific, he will also make his subject matter more palatable to those who may approach it.

The precise formulation of chemical and physical changes pertains to the purely physical sciences. Linguistics is not a purely physical science. It is a study of language, which is a human activity, carried on by living human beings and subject to human vicissitudes.

The question of taste in language is in part tied up with literature and stylistic standards. It is self-evident that while everyone is able to use language for purposes of ordinary communication, not everyone is able to use it for purposes of great literature or oratory. It is perhaps one of the tragedies of the world of education that instead of training everyone to express his meaning clearly and understandably, the attempt has consistently been at turning into literary critics and poets people who have neither the ability nor the inclination for those pursuits.

The literary, esthetic aspects of language are essentially aristocratic; the communicative aspects essentially democratic and universal. The sooner this is realized, the sooner we shall achieve some real results in our educational process, particularly for what concerns language. Not everyone can be trained to understand and appreciate the literary values of Shakespeare and Dante; but everyone can be trained to speak, understand, read and write for purposes of ordinary life and ordinary communication.

This proposition leads in turn to another thorny question: what language standards are to be imparted for the latter purpose? Shall the best, or the worst standards of language be taught? Here the issue of taste links up with that of usage, which will be discussed a little later.

NOTES TO PROBLEM X

1. See M. Pei, *The Story of Language,* Philadelphia, 1949, pp. 254–255; *One Language for the World,* New York, 1958, pp. 96–105.

2. K. Nyrop, *Grammaire historique de la langue française,* 1901–1903, p. 34.

3. Iordan and Orr, *op. cit.,* pp. 115–120.

4. As a single, simple refutation of this stultifying point of view, take the case of Russian *ravvin* for "rabbi." Why do the Russians use this form with a *vv* when the original Hebrew and most other languages have *bb*? Is it simply because they have been saying it that way for one thousand years? Or is it because the word came into Slavic from Greek, which had used *beta* to transcribe the Hebrew *beth*? This *beta,* pronounced by the Greeks as a *b* when they had borrowed the word, had changed its sound to that of *v* by the time the Greek missionaries christianized the Slavs. The latter, hearing the Greek word as *ravvi,* not *rabbi,* turned it into *ravvin,* and the "error," if we want to call it that, has not yet been rectified.

5. See R. A. Hall, Jr.'s review of my *Italian Language* in *Language,* 17.3 (1941), pp. 263–269; W. D. Elcock, *The Romance Languages,* Macmillan, New York, 1960, p. 35.

6. W. von Wartburg, *Die Ausgliederung der romanischen Sprachräume,* Bern, Francke, 1950 (see also review by R. Politzer, *Romanic Review,* XLII, 3 [Oct. 1951], pp. 230–235); G. Devoto, *Storia della lingua di Roma,* Bologna, 1940, p. 296 f. See also my review in *Romanic Review,* XXXIV, 2 (April 1943), pp. 184–189. Von Wartburg's earlier *La Posizione della lingua italiana,* Firenze, 1940, also presents some interesting considerations on this topic.

Languages in Contact

THE issue of languages in contact is a recent one. It may be said to have had its inception in the nineteenth century, when the writers of the Neolinguist school, and particularly the Italian G. I. Ascoli brought it to the fore.[1]

It is the contention of the followers of this school that if a given language overspreads the area once held by another, as was the case with Latin in Gaul, Iberia, and most of Italy, its further development in that area will be affected by the linguistic habits of the earlier group. The latter forms an ethnical substratum, or racial underlayer, and even though their language vanishes, it leaves its trace, in certain modified habits, particularly of pronunciation, that affect the invading language for what concerns the area in question. If later invaders arrive, and give up their own language in favor of the one they find, they, too, may contribute certain habits of speech to the ultimate language of the area.

This ethnical substratum and superstratum theory[2] has been advanced to account for a multitude of language phenomena. It has been suggested, for example, that the Germanic consonant shift whereby the *p* of *pater* turns into the *f* of *father*, the *d* of *dentem* into the *t* of *tooth*, etc., is due to the language habits of earlier inhabitants in the Germanic area; that Armenian was influenced in its sound scheme by the sound scheme of the nearby Caucasian languages; that the syntactical peculiarities of Old Irish are partly due to an earlier Iberian or Berber substratum; that the retroflex consonants of Sanskrit are borrowed from the Dravidian languages of India; that the unusual development of vowels in Dalmatian (Vegliote) was due to the influence of nearby Serbo-Croatian; etc.

Where the substratum theory has been most extensively advanced, however, is in the field of Romance development, where it has been used to account for divergences among Romance tongues stemming from what is in appearance a uniform Latin. Ascoli, for example, suggests in his *Saggi ladini* that the middle rounded *ü* sound, appearing, as it does, in areas where Gaulish was once spoken (France, northwestern Italy, portions of Switzerland) stems from Celtic habits of pronunciation, preserved through the long period of Romanization. Friedrich Diez, fifty years earlier, had suggested the possibility that the Spanish change of initial *f-* to *h-* might be due to Basque-Iberian reluctance to pronounce the *f* sound. Certain sounds appearing in the southern Italian dialects have in like manner been attributed to Oscan speech habits, while the Etruscans have been blamed for the Tuscan habit of aspirating certain Italian consonant sounds.

The substratum theory was especially fashionable in the later years of the nineteenth century and the early decades of the twentieth, being in part supplemented, in part complemented by the kindred superstratum theory. (Von Wartburg, for instance, attributes the diphthongization of vowels in open syllables in French and Italian to the speech habits of the Franks and the Longobards, respectively.) [3]

The term adstratum was originally coined to cover both substratum and superstratum, as well as to account for the influence exerted upon the receiving language by a contributing language that does not itself disappear (as in the case of Basque contributing the *f* to *h* change to Castilian).

Of late, it has become the vogue to speak not so much of adstratum as of languages in contact.[4] Here the theory is that languages of different origins, coexisting in the same area, will develop certain common features, particularly in syntax, not so much by a process of outright borrowing as by one of unconscious imitation, induced by that coexistence in an identical environment. An example of this would be the fact that three Balkan languages, Rumanian (a Romance tongue), Bulgarian (a Slavic or Slavicized language), and Albanian (a language representing a separate branch of Indo-European) all have in common the suffixation of the definite article to the noun. A further example might perhaps be supplied by the *-s* plural of English, which has practically supplanted all the other plural formations that were common in Anglo-Saxon as they are in modern German or Scandinavian (*feet, oxen, deer* are a few stray survivals). Could this triumph of the *-s* plural, comparatively rare in Anglo-Saxon, be due to the long coexistence of English and French on English soil after the Norman Conquest? (In Old French the oblique plural forms of masculine nouns, and practically all feminine plurals, end in *-s*.)

There is no doubt that the substratum-superstratum-adstratum contact theories hold many attractive and plausible features. To begin with, no linguist will deny that they are completely operative for what concerns one of the great divisions of language, vocabulary. Spanish and Portuguese have Basque, Iberian and Arabic words which the other Romance languages lack. French has a heavier percentage of both Gaulish and Frankish words. Italian has borrowed from Ostrogothic, Longobardic, and from the ancient languages of Italy. Rumanian has taken many words from Slavic, Turkish, Byzantine Greek and Hungarian. French words have gotten into English, Arabic words into Turkish, Persian and Urdu, Chinese words into Japanese and Korean, and so on ad infinitum. The process of word-borrowing among languages goes on apace today.

But the essence of the substratum and kindred theories is not the borrowing of words, but the borrowing of sounds and sound schemes, and, to a lesser degree, of grammatical devices. It is here that the controversy arises.

It has been repeatedly pointed out that the various substratum phenomenon in the field of language sounds are susceptible of different explanations. The range of phonological change is vast, but nevertheless limited. The possibility of stray coincidence is always there to haunt us. The alternation of *f* and *h* that appears in Basque and Castilian appears also in Japanese, in Sicilian, Calabrian, and some of the ancient dialects of Italy (Faliscan *haba, hircus,* for Latin *faba, fircus*) ; it does not occur to the linguists to suggest an influence exerted by Japanese or Faliscan on Spanish because the languages have never been in contact, as Basque and Castilian are. Transitions from *u* to *i,* through an intermediate *ü* stage, are extremely frequent, in all sorts of languages, including Latin (*optumus, maxumus* to *optimus, maximus*). Is it altogether necessary to attribute the French and north Italian *ü* to a Celtic substratum, particularly in view of the fact that no reference to such a sound appears in the writings of Latin grammarians, some of whom were Gallo-Romans? The transition from Latin to Italian shows such phenomena of retrogressive assimilation as *pt* and *kt* to *tt;* so does the transition from Sanskrit to the Prakrits. It is true that Balkan languages such as Rumanian, Bulgarian and Albanian have a suffixated definite article; but so do the Scandinavian languages; if no common link is suggested between the two groups, in view of their geographical separation, why must we necessarily assume a common link among the Balkan tongues?

French and Italian display completely different types of palatalization of c before e and i (in Italian, the original k sound of Latin turns into the sound of English ch; in French, into the sound of ts, later modified into the sound of s). In addition, French, but not Italian, palatalizes c before a into the sound of English ch, later modified into the sound of English sh. There is one dialect of French, Picard, that behaves in this respect precisely like Italian. Had Picard been located near the Italian border, no power on earth could have stopped the substratum theorists from assuming a link or an influence between the Italian and the Picard phenomena. But Picard happens to be spoken at the opposite end of France, so the rash assumption has not been made.

It has been established that differences of pronunciation in the various types of American Spanish, once thought to be due to the substratum influence of the American Indian languages, all represent importations from different localities in Spain.[5] It has also been established that a Gallo-Italian dialect from the north of Italy, whose speakers were transplanted in the Middle Ages to Sicily, borrowed extensively in the field of vocabulary from the surrounding Sicilian dialects, but practically not at all for what concerns the sound pattern.[6]

All this does not mean that the ethnical substratum theory should be discarded a priori. Indeed, it should be, and is, recognized as fully valid for what concerns vocabulary and, to some extent, syntactical arrangements (the earliest document of Gothic, Wulfila's translation of the Bible, is filled with Greek syntactical arrangements). It simply means that in the field of phonological development and phonemic patterns it is still largely unproved.

If operative, it is so to a small and doubtful degree. The conflicting evidence in each individual case has to be reweighed and revalued in order to establish the probable truth of each separate proposition.

NOTES TO PROBLEM XI

1. "Saggi ladini," *Archivio Glottologico Italiano*, I, VIII.

2. Iordan and Orr, *op. cit.*, p. 12, n. 1; M. Pei, *The Story of Language*, pp. 149–150; *Language for Everybody*, New York, 1957, pp. 146–151.

3. See Problem X, n. 6.

4. U. Weinrich, *Languages in Contact*, New York, 1953.

5. W. J. Entwistle, *The Spanish Language*, New York, 1938, pp. 72, 230–250.

6. M. B. Finocchiaro, *The Gallo-Italian Dialect of Nicosia*, New York, 1950.

Meaning in Language

LANGUAGE in its outer, formal manifestations is a highly relative phenomenon. It can assume a multiplicity of forms. It can make or fail to make certain distinctions, which will be paramount to one language, irrelevant to another.

The *purpose* of language is absolute. It is the transfer of meaning from one human mind to another. If the form of communication used fails in this one respect, no true language can be said to exist.

The fact that many other devices besides speech serve the purpose of meaningful transfer has perhaps obscured the issue, and led some linguists to deny the name of language to such items as writing, gesture, facial expression, semaphores and signals of all sorts. This is mainly a question of terminology and, in a sense, unimportant.

Even if we restrict the term "language" to the point where it becomes synonymous with speech, the fact still remains that the purpose of speech is absolute and unchangeable. If speech does not carry meaning, if there is no semantic transfer from one mind to another, speech resolves itself into a series of noises produced through the instrumentality of the human vocal apparatus, transmitted along the air waves, perhaps received by a human ear, but incapable of being referred to the thought centers for interpretation. We can call these noises "language" if we like, but in effect they will differ not at all from any other natural or artificial noises.

Meaning is a community of understanding, so that for the time being you and I think in the same terms. If this fails to happen, we may as well "save our breath," as the saying goes, and reserve it for more practical purposes, such as to get oxygen into our lungs and get rid of the carbon dioxide in our system.

It is therefore strange to encounter a school of linguistics that eschews meaning in its analysis of language, basing the latter solely on form and function. A certain sequence of sounds behaves in a certain characteristic way, say the members of this school, and this is all we need to know to classify our sequence correctly and establish our language categories in the tongue under consideration. The connotation that the sound sequence itself may evoke in the minds of the speakers of the language is unimportant.[1]

In proof of this, they submit sentences formed of nonsense words, which nevertheless conform to the sound structure and the grammatical pattern of the language, sentences such as "Saric ronings teld benning lorts." Here everything is in accordance with the English sound pattern and grammatical structure. The sounds are English sounds, and their sequence follows the normal sequence for English, with syllables generally ending in consonants, and consonant clusters of the type that English admits and favors.

Grammatically, *saric,* by virtue of the fact that it ends in *-ic* and that it precedes another word which is evidently a noun (for reasons that will become clear in a minute), is a modifier, or what the older school of grammarians would describe as an adjective. *Ronings* seems to be built on a root *ron-,* with an *-ing* suffix, which is of participial origin and can therefore be used as an adjective or as a noun; but the fact that in this particular situation it is followed by *-s,* normally a plural suffix, would imply a noun function. *Teld* is by itself noncommittal, but it comes in the normal position for an English verb, and its form, without final -*s*, would seem to work well with the assumed "noun" *ronings* which acts as its subject. *Benning* again has the -*ing* ending characteristic of participles; but this time its use before *lorts* would seem to imply an adjectival function. *Lorts,* by its position and ending, works out very well as a plural noun. Since *ronings* with its assumed modifier comes before *teld,* while *lorts,* with its modifier, follows *teld,* one may assume that *ronings* is the doer of the action implied by *teld, lorts* its receiver. The entire nonsense sentence could now be replaced by one that makes sense: "Slavic endings show recurring patterns."

The sentence is now "analyzed," and the unknown meaning of each of the five words has never once come into play.

The assumption was that we already knew the grammatical structure of English, and made use of our knowledge in "analyzing" the nonsense sentence. But the procedure can be put in reverse when dealing with a language of which the grammatical structure is unknown. We then examine a large number of sentences, and from the behavior of the individual units as exemplified over and over again we proceed to establish the grammatical rules. But here we run into a snag.

Suppose a man who sees or hears English for the first time is faced with an array of sentences of this type:

"The king sees."
"The kings see."
"The boy sings."
"The boys sing."
"The girl walks."
"The girls walk."
"The student speaks."
"The students speak."

He may, after much puzzling, be able to figure out that the

invariable *the* is an article, that the following word is a noun, that nouns take -*s* in the plural, that the third word in each sentence is a verb, that verbs take -*s* in the third singular but no -*s* in the third plural. But the chances are against it, unless he has a key to the meaning.

Actually, this is precisely the situation that stymies our research in Etruscan. The researchers have been able to figure some of the forms and, to some extent, the grammatical structure of the language.[2] What they lack is the meaning of the words, and until a new Rosetta Stone with a lengthy bilingual inscription comes to light, the chances are that the Etruscan language will continue to be a mystery. All the vaunted linguistic analysis based on form and function divorced from meaning is of no avail. It is no wonder that followers of the form-minus-meaning school, when they undertake to investigate an American Indian language, provide themselves with one or more informants who can give them the English meanings of the native words, or at least of the native sentences.

Transfer of meaning is the basic purpose of language, and the association between language and meaning is indissoluble. There is, however, another phase of language and meaning that is independent of transfer, or, to put it more precisely, independent of universal transfer. It is a known fact that in each language there are words and expressions that are untranslatable into other tongues, save through a process of circumlocution, explanation and definition. It is extremely difficult, for example, to render into a Romance language, at least by a one-for-one translation, the connotations conveyed in English "home" or "pet." Neither "house" nor "domestic fireside" will precisely convey the first, with its overtones, nor will "domestic animal" or "dear little beast" take care of the second. The present writer was once asked, for purposes of a jacket design, to translate into a number of assorted languages the title (not selected by himself) of one of his own books, *All About Language.* It was easy enough to translate "about," but no language except English would tolerate "all" in front of it and still make sense. In like manner, there is no rendering the German *Weltschmerz* or *Sehnsucht,* the Portuguese *saudades,* the French *épatant,* the Spanish *ojalá*—at least, not by using a single English word. Each language has, in the course of its history, evolved a series of special psychological associations for various words and expressions in its vocabulary which other languages do not share.

This is perhaps the reason why some linguists look askance upon the idea of an international language, and say that a language represents a culture, and that until we have achieved a world culture we cannot achieve a world language. The world culture seems to be definitely on its way, but even before it is achieved, there is nothing wrong with achieving an international tongue that will serve the basic purpose of material transfer of meaning. Once it is in operation, it will hasten the process of standardizing the world's cultures, if that is what is desired.

To think that at the outset a world language will be able to gather within itself all the delicate overtones and shades of meaning conveyed today by some (by no means all) words in the various languages is an illusion, and that is why the international language should be advocated on its merits as a tool of purely material communication, not of that peculiar, illusory thing known as "understanding."

Understanding in the sense in which some people use it does not exist even among the speakers of the same language. "Democracy" and "liberty" mean different things not merely to Americans and Russians, but even among Americans to the exclusion of Russians. It will be a sorry day indeed when all abstract terms mean exactly the same thing to all men, because on that day human beings will have lost their human quality of individualism. Each person must necessarily refer language symbols to his own experience, and no two of us have the same background of experience.

Even where the term represents approximately the same concept to two different human minds, the reaction may be altogether different. "Profits" may be understood to mean pretty much the same thing by both the shareholder and the labor union member, but the former has been trained to surround the term with a halo of pleasant associations, the latter has seen it excoriated and surrounded by such modifiers as "fat," "bloated," "extortionate." To one it is sweet music, to the other the clang of chains. The description of a rich, tasty dish may cause your mouth to water if you are healthy and hungry, but may bring on an attack of nausea if you are suffering from seasickness. Let us therefore beware of the siren song of the semanticists, general and otherwise, who urge that words shall have the same meaning under all circumstances and to all men.

Meaning, like its carrier, language, is subject to human variability and human differences. It is as vain to speak of regimenting meaning as it is to speak of regimenting language. Neither will submit to iron-bound laws. But both will and do show tendencies, areas of general agreement, which permit the business of semantic transfer to go on and function, not as a machine functions, but as a human being functions.

Language cannot be divorced from meaning, even for purposes of so-called scientific analysis. Neither language nor meaning can be strait-jacketed. But this does not mean that anarchy must reign. Order, and orderly progress, can coexist with a measure (and quite a large one) of individual freedom and personal choice.

NOTES TO PROBLEM XII

1. For the peculiar procedure outlined in this chapter, see *Readings in Applied English Linguistics,* ed. H. B. Allen: "Meaning and Language Analysis," by C. C. Fries, pp. 101–113, and particularly "Resolution of Structural Ambiguity by Lexical Probability," by W. N. Francis, pp. 114–118 ("He darbed the vellig a harnip").

2. M. Pallottino, *Elementi di lingua etrusca,* Firenze, 1936.

Authority vs. Usage

(THIS chapter is to some extent repetitive of what appears in Problem II. The considerations here advanced, however, bear on the practical and pedagogical aspects of language rather than the philosophical.)

Prescriptive grammarians are practically as old as man's consciousness of language. A glance at our historical survey will indicate that Sanskrit and Greek grammarians codified the structure of their languages to the best of their ability, and presumably with reference to the best standard usage of their times. The prescriptive grammatical habit, passed on by the Greeks to the Romans, then gave rise to our medieval and modern grammars. Latin supplied the standard procedure.

We are all acquainted with the abuses of grammarians. Striding unopposed in a field in which they were supreme, they legislated as they saw fit. Some of their prescriptions are antiquated, others absurd. (As an all-time sample of absurdity, the reader is referred to Fowler's *The King's English,* where our traditional grammarian, after prescribing to his heart's content on each point at issue, cites long lists of "mistakes" appearing in the most famous writers of the English language, from Shakespeare to De Quincey and from Macaulay to Dickens.) It is little wonder that this combination of anachronism and lack of common sense gave rise to a reaction.

Linguists of the younger generation, particularly in America, gave the signal of revolt against traditional grammar and its abuses. Beginning with Bloomfield's famous statement to the effect that "our schools and colleges teach us very little about language, and what little they teach us is largely in error,"[1] and continuing through some of the pronouncements made in the very recent past,[2] we have an entire literature on the subject.

The doctrine of usage began to be advanced. "Language is what people speak, not what someone thinks they ought to speak" was the motto of the new school. But usage presents its own peculiar problems. What usage? Whose usage? In a country speaking what appears on the surface to be a fairly unified language, like the United States, there are innumerable levels of usage and innumerable local varieties of speech. To a certain extent, it is possible to list and catalogue the variants, though many of them manage to escape notice.[3]

But language has its practical as well as its theoretical problems. What shall we present, particularly for purposes of instruction, as the standard language of a given country, or even of a given area? In attempting to present an entity that empirically does not exist, such as "American English," how shall we go about describing the phonetic and phonemic differences displayed by the various regions? Or their grammatical peculiarities? Or their divergences of vocabulary and semantics? The identical problem arises over and over again as we approach each language, whether it be large or small.

The old prescriptive grammarians were not faced with any such problem. They set up the standard themselves, then arrogantly proceeded to label every divergence from it an "error." Obviously, if language is what people actually speak and not what someone orders them to speak, there are no "errors." Each native speaker is justified in doing exactly what he pleases. To be thoroughly consistent, the same freedom ought to apply to each foreign learner of the language. Confusion can be compounded as well as confounded.

It is customary for reformers in all fields to make sweeping pronouncements, then to modify them to suit the circumstances. In the field of language, we have seen that happen with the proponents of the iron-bound sound laws and their analogical escape hatch. In the matter of usage and grammar, the same hedging has become more and more evident. First we have the setting up of separate "standard" and "substandard" speakers, a division into sheep and goats, which does not differ materially from the old "correct" and "incorrect" labels. Next we have the creation of what amounts to a new grammar, applicable at first only to English, then extended to cover a new concept of universality.

Whorf, in one of his essays, hinted at the possibility of constructing such a grammar. The modern linguists have actually gone to work and produced one. If we carefully examine one of the most recent works in the field of linguistics, Hockett's,[4] we shall find a full-blown set of brand-new grammatical terminologies and grammatical distinctions, largely exemplified from English, but basically applicable, with appropriate modifications, to most languages.

This means that we are back where we started. The doctrine of usage, which in practice amounts to letting each speaker do what he pleases, is circumscribed by the appendage of standard vs. substandard language. The range of permissiveness is somewhat different (allowance is made, for instance, for certain localisms), but the difference is of degree rather than kind. Secondly, grammar is not at all discarded. It is rather rebuilt, with a few rather minor modifications, and a brand-new terminology. Emphasis is shifted here and there, particularly in connection with the description of sounds, which are far more thoroughly (even ultra-accurately) described in the new system than they were in the old. (Note, for instance, the stress on intonation and juncture, something which old-style grammars, approaching language from the written angle, largely ignored.) When it comes to a description of the morphemic structure of the language (what old-style grammarians would describe as morphology and syntax, the core of "grammar"), the advantages of the new system are questionable.

For this there is a reason. Shorn of silly, artificial distinctions (such as the use of *shall* and *will* in English), our old system of grammatical concepts and parts of speech is based primarily on formal distinctions, the very thing the new grammarians advocate. There is no denying that the terminology of Sanskrit, Greek and Latin grammar is supremely suited to the structure of those languages, and to the distinctions of form and function appearing in them. Traditional grammar is not so much Sanskrit, or Greek, or Latin, as it is common Indo-European. Avowedly, its terminology and procedure are best suited for those modern languages, like Russian, which have best preserved the old Indo-European structure. But it is also largely applicable, with a few necessary modifications, to languages like English or French, which have given up some of the old morphological trappings, but by no means all. Nouns, adjectives, pronouns, verbs are still fully identifiable as such by reference to their form and function combined. It is perhaps unnecessary to transplant the entire terminology of Latin grammar into English, but there are enough vestigial remains of the ancient structure, even in modern American English, to justify the use of most of it. English presents gender distinctions, if not in nouns, at least in pronouns. Number, tense, voice are still there, even if the distinction of mood is largely effaced. Enough of a case system endures to permit us to speak logically of a nominative, accusative and genitive. If functional change is unaccompanied by formal distinctions, cannot the fact be stated? And is it quite true that functional change is unaccompanied by formal distinctions? "He upped me five dollars"; "the ups and downs of life"; "I mailed the book"; here the one-time preposition takes on verbal or noun endings, and the one-time noun takes on the characteristic endings of a verb.

The old-style grammarians used to be fond of the twin processes of parsing and diagramming. Examine Hockett,[5] and see how these processes are continued in modern dress. Also, compare the two systems and determine which you prefer, for practical or pedagogical purposes.

The fact of the matter is that in order to have any sort of orderly description of language, we must have: 1. a standard (call it the Voice of Authority, or the Academy, or the vague "standard speech" of the modern linguists, or by any other name you please); 2. a set of rules or traffic regulations (call it traditional grammar, or phonemic and morphemic description, or something else).

The new system of grammar evolved by the American school of linguistics has some undoubted merits; it also has some decided disadvantages, not the least of which is the overcomplication of its terminology and the establishment of distinctions drawn so fine that they are of no practical use. (The juncture phenomena exemplified in "lighthousekeeper" vs. "light housekeeper," or in "white house" vs. "White House" are cases in point.)

Is the old-style grammar worth saving? Of course, it must be shorn of its absurdities, which are the product of individuals rather than faults in the system, and brought up to date for each individual language. To it must be added those innovations of modern linguistics which have truly proved their worth.

Outside of this, a defense of traditional grammar is possible not merely on the basis of traditionalism, but on that of utilitarianism.

Traditional grammar and its traditional terminology are well suited to Indo-European languages, particularly those which have largely retained the ancient structure. With a few modifications, they can still serve, and serve well, the modern Indo-European tongues which have gone through a process of evolution. Medieval and Renaissance grammarians found no difficulty in applying their traditional grammar to those non-Indo-European tongues with which they were in contact, because both Semitic tongues, like Hebrew and Arabic, and Ural-Altaic tongues, like Turkish and Hungarian, have enough structural similarity to Indo-European to permit a transfer. This means that our old grammatical concepts and terminology can be applied to tongues spoken by roughly three-fourths of the earth's population. That a transfer of terminology and grammatical method can be effected with other large groups is proved by the semi-traditional treatment, applied by the upholders of the "new grammar" themselves, to Far Eastern languages like Japanese and Chinese.[6] An African language like Swahili submits quite gracefully to traditional terminology.

The languages that do not submit gracefully are, in the main, those of the American Indians, beloved of the American linguistic scientists. In many of these the pattern is so different that the application of traditional grammatical concepts is either difficult or impossible.

The question then arises whether we must discard all of our old apparatus, which has served us and continues to serve us well, because it cannot be utilized in connection with a few minor groups that represent little in actual numbers and still less in standards of civilization.

NOTES TO PROBLEM XIII

1. L. Bloomfield, *Outline Guide for the Practical Study of Foreign Languages,* Baltimore, 1942, p. 1.

2. *Readings in Applied English Linguistics,* p. 209 (J. B. McMillan): "The traditional superstitious identification of the 'rules' of English grammar with the 'rules' of a mythical 'good English' must go"; p. 113 (C. C. Fries): "the superstitions of the past"; p. 349 (M. Burnet): "language superstitions."

3. The best attempt to date, in my estimation, is A. Bronstein's *The Pronunciation of American English,* Appleton-Century-Crofts, New York, 1960.

4. C. Hockett, *Course in Modern Linguistics,* Macmillan, New York, 1958.

5. Hockett, *op. cit.,* pp. 147–208.

6. See, for example, M. G. Tewsbury, *Spoken Chinese,* Yale University Press, New Haven, 1948; he speaks of nouns, verbs, adverbs, particles, modifiers, auxiliary verbs, and brings in, where needed, such specifically Chinese concepts as stative verbs, specifiers, measures, etc.

The Spoken vs. the Written Language

(AGAIN, some of the points made here have already appeared in Problem VII. But again, it is the practical, pedagogical aspects rather than the philosophical or historical that are stressed here.)

The fact that the word "grammar" is built on the root of the Greek word that means "to write" is in itself an indication of the veneration with which the ancients regarded the written word, and of the intimate link that existed in their minds between writing and grammar. The Roman saying *Verba volant, scripta manent* ("Words fly away, but what is written remains") is another clue. The numerous ancient legends concerning the divine origin of writing (the Egyptians, for example, believed that writing had been bestowed upon the human race by Thoth, the god of wisdom) are a third.

Writing, down to the beginning of the present century, enjoyed two distinct advantages over speech: it could transmit language at a distance, and it was permanent. Speech could not overcome barriers of time and space; writing could.

It goes without saying that in these days of disk, tape and wire recordings, telegraph cables and telephone wires, radio, TV and spoken films, these advantages no longer exist. We can, if we choose, make the spoken message permanent and transmit it at great distances.

As far back as the 1930's, Bloomfield expressed the hope that "mechanical devices for reproducing speech will supersede our present habits of writing and printing."[1] At a somewhat later date, E. H. Sturtevant suggested that "the most efficient as well as the easiest way to improve the situation would be the complete cessation of the teaching of spelling."[2] I myself have envisaged, though without glee, the possibility that writing may one day disappear, and all communications across time and space be conducted by means of "canned" speech, in one form or another.[3]

At the same time, it is only fair to add that if writing is on its way out, it has never displayed such vitality as in its final days. Giant strides have been made and are being made to eliminate illiteracy, and the mass of written and printed records of all kinds has never been so great as it is today. Whatever the future may hold in store for the written language, it would be quite unsafe to neglect it at present, just as it would be unsafe to scrap our railroads, automobiles and ships on the ground that they are about to be superseded by planes, helicopters and rockets.

The present-day problem of speech vs. writing has two facets, a practical and a scientific one. On the practical side, for purposes of language instruction, both in the native and in foreign tongues, it is argued by many that writing is purely secondary; that the only "true" form of language is speech, and that we are not even justified in speaking of the "written language."[4] In terms of instruction, this means that the spoken tongue, with all its vagaries and uncertainties, is revered, while the written tongue, which is usually far more definite, stable and standardized, is regarded as unimportant, something that you can take or leave alone. Grammars based on the written language, which is normally a country's "official" language, are decried as unrealistic (some of them are, because they are based not on the universal modern standard, but on the antiquated language of literature) ; new grammars, based exclusively on the spoken tongue, are constructed; literature itself is viewed as the aristocratic, spiritual vehicle of expression of the chosen few (which indeed it is), and as having little or no link with speech, the democratic means of material communication of the multitudes.

Reflections of this attitude are evident in the neglect of spelling, punctuation and grammar current in our schools, as well as in the reluctance of the younger generations to read and write, particularly the latter. (It is so much easier to pick up the phone and talk!)

Viewing this practical problem realistically and unemotionally, it can only be said that while the omens for the future may point in the direction of the disappearance of writing, such disappearance is not at all in evidence at the present time. For a person of the living generations, illiteracy is not recommended. Far too many purely practical situations still depend on the written medium (signs, menus, newspapers, directions are a few cases in point). Even if the world's future records are destined to consist of canned speech, the world's past records, down to the end of the nineteenth century, appear almost exclusively in written form.

In addition, the Roman *Verba volant, scripta manent* holds a hidden as well as an overt meaning. The written language is something you can take at your own speed, hastening the reading or slowing it down, according to circumstances, pausing to reflect on what you have read to extract the recondite content, if any, savoring it to the full if there is anything to savor. It is possible, of course, to halt or backspace a recording, but it is not quite the same thing. Listen to one of Shakespeare's plays on the stage, or on a recording, then read it. Unless you are quite extraordinary, you will note that the reading brings out points that are overlooked in the audition.

For what concerns the scientific facet, the quarrel lies between those who attribute paramount importance to written records in connection with linguistic phenomena and development, and those who view such records with skepticism and disbelief, as not illustrating the true course of the spoken tongue. Here opinions range all the way from denying all validity to written documents as a reflection of the spoken language to acceptance of such evidence as fully valid, with only such divergences as are inherent in the two forms and directly observable in the case of present-day languages.[5]

It may be stressed that the controversy is almost purely a twentieth-century affair. As has already been pointed out in Problem VII, the historical linguists of the past accepted at face value all inscriptional and textual material, and those of the present continue to do so for what concerns languages such as Hittite, Akkadian, Gothic, Gaulish, etc., which have not survived into the present in modified form. In fact, it is almost possible to restrict the controversy to the field of the languages descended from Latin. Here the stream of textual material is continuous and unbroken, leading by easy stages from archaic and pre-Classical Latin to the works of standard Latin literature, then, through the post-Classical output, into the texts of the fourth to the eighth centuries, described by some as Vulgar Latin, by others as primitive Romance, then on into material that is definitely on the Romance side of the linguistic divide.

Since Latin, in a more or less Classical form, continued to be a spoken language in scholarly circles throughout the Middle Ages and the early Renaissance, the question is at what point did the written language cease to be a reflection of the spoken popular tongue of the illiterate or semi-literate masses, even with all due allowance made for the normal spread between speech and writing.

Believers in the validity of the written language are of the opinion that the mass of documents and inscriptions from the controversial centuries contain, if properly read and evaluated, the evidence we may legitimately expect for the progression of the spoken tongue. Opponents of this view interpret divergences from Classical standards appearing in this evidence to be merely indications of growing ignorance of Latin on the part of scribes and stonecutters who were speaking something quite different.[6] For the progression and development of the spoken tongue of the period under consideration, followers of the second school prefer a process of hypothetical reconstruction similar to that employed for Indo-European, but supplemented by evidence supplied by present-day languages and dialects as recorded in the linguistic atlases.

Obviously, it is impossible to enter here into the numerous arguments and elements of proof advanced by the two sides, whose lines are at any rate not very clearly drawn.[7]

There is no doubt that the reconstruction process is easier, since it calls only for a series of extended comparisons from modern spoken tongues and dialects, plus almost mathematical equations and formulas. The textual process means not merely delving into an extraordinarily large quantity of texts and inscriptions, some of which are difficult to decipher, but interpreting the phenomena appearing in them, which in turn means going into detectivelike processes of induction and deduction. The results of this painstaking research are, however, often richly rewarding, since new material is forever coming to light. Often the findings of the textual researcher confirm those of the reconstructor; occasionally the two are in direct conflict.

It is here that collaboration ceases and professional intolerance begins. "It is difficult to believe that things were so, in spite of all the available evidence" is the comment of one a priori theorist to a mass of documentary evidence submitted to him. The attitude of many others is: "We know that things were so. We have figured it all out. If your documents are in contrast with our findings, the documents lie."

This attitude is, to say the least, unscientific. It betokens a pessimistic state of mind which abandons the search in advance, and substitutes dogma for scientific proof.

If the documents of a given period do not reflect the spoken language, at what point does the cleavage between speech and writing occur? The extremists of the reconstructive school will reply that the cleavage was always there, that nowhere and at no time is writing a reflection of speech. If this is so, we may as well bid farewell to all our comparative studies on earlier languages, which are based exclusively on written forms. It is tantamount to saying that the only languages we can be sure of are those spoken in our own times, and for which it is possible to secure the testimony of living speakers.

Others hedge by pushing back the time of cleavage, some to the Classical, others to the pre-Classical period. For this procedure there is neither evidence nor advantage. Historical research, to be accurate, calls for the full utilization of all sources of evidence, documentary and inscriptional, the stray remarks of writers and grammarians, Latin loan words appearing in other languages, and even, but not exclusively, modern linguistic geography and the process of comparative reconstruction.

But this angle of the problem is of interest only to a few linguistic specialists. The other, that of handling the current written language with the respect that is due it, is of interest to each and every one of us. In fact, it is the major problem of modern education, particularly in America.

While the written language endures, it must be neither neglected nor mishandled, under penalty of plunging our nation back into the semi-literacy that prevailed throughout recorded history, almost down to the end of the nineteenth century.[8]

NOTES TO PROBLEM XIV

1. L. Bloomfield, *Language,* Holt, New York, 1933, p. 503.

2. E. H. Sturtevant, *Introduction to Linguistic Science,* Yale University Press, New Haven, 1947, p. 25.

3. M. Pei, *The Story of English,* Lippincott, Philadelphia, 1952, pp. 278–281.

4. Hockett, *op. cit.,* p. 4.

5. See Problem VII, notes 3, 4.

6. See J. Vielliard, *La Langue des diplômes royaux et chartes privées de l'époque mérovingienne,* Paris, 1927, pp. ix, 38; M. Pei, *The Language of the Eighth-Century Texts in Northern France,* New York, 1932, pp. 356–363.

7. See Problem VII, notes 3, 4; also Elcock, *op. cit.;* Pei, *The Italian Language.*

8. It must not be forgotten that at the outset of the nineteenth century literacy in America and in the most advanced countries of western Europe was only about 20 per cent (roughly, the same percentage that had existed for the previous 2,000 years). By 1860, it had risen to perhaps 40 per cent, by 1900 to 80 per cent. Complete or almost complete literacy, even for countries like the United States, Great Britain, France, Germany, is definitely a twentieth-century phenomenon. See M. Pei, *The Story of Language,* pp. 278–284.

The International Language

THE arguments on behalf of *an* international language, as apart from some specific language, national or constructed, such as English or Esperanto, have been fully set forth elsewhere.[1]

The point at issue is not whether it would be better to have a constructed language or a national tongue for international use, or whether English would serve the purpose better than French, or Interlingua better than Esperanto. The question is whether a language (*any* language), set apart for universal use by all the world's inhabitants, or, at any rate, by those among them who have access to schooling, would be desirable.

In such a discussion, we should leave out of consideration the claims so often advanced that an international language would lead to greater understanding, friendship and peace among the nations, since history has abundantly proved that this is not necessarily so. We should also, temporarily, leave out of the discussion the question of which language would be most suitable, or how such a language should be chosen. We should put the horse before the cart, and begin at the beginning: do we want an international language at all, or do we prefer to go along the way we are?

The international language, at this stage, should be viewed purely as a tool of communication, like language itself. Will we be able to communicate better with such a tool? Will it smooth our path and facilitate our activities, whatever these may be?

Historically, the question was given no serious consideration until the seventeenth century. Classical antiquity took it for granted that Latin and Greek were fully international tongues. The Middle Ages were satisfied with the Latin of scholarship, at least for what concerned western Europe. It was only when nationalism in the modern sense began to lift its head, and the vernaculars had gotten to usurp the place of international diplomatic and governmental Latin, that the idea occurred to Descartes and numerous others to create a language that would serve the purpose of international exchanges. The early linguistic internationalists, being philosophically trained, were overconcerned with the question of logic in their creations, utterly forgetting that language, in its natural state, is anything but logical. This led to needless complexities and widespread rejection. But the nineteenth century came to the rescue with constructed languages that stressed ease to the learner rather than logic. Ease to the learner meant ease to that part of the world's population which really counted in those days; in other words, people who either spoke Western type languages as mother tongues, or had fully assimilated them. Therefore, everything constructed along lines of "ease" is a compromise of Latin, Greek, Romance and Germanic, in different blends. This goes on into the present, as shown by such twentieth-century creations as Jespersen's *Novial,* Peano's *Latino Sine Flexione,* and the very recent American-built *Interlingua.*

That language does not have to be logical to be effective as a tool of communication is proved by every natural language in existence. That it does not have to be made "easy" for anyone, save adult foreign learners whose language habits are already set, is proved by the fact that Russian and Chinese children learn to speak their languages as easily as American children learn theirs, as well as by the very large number of people who are thoroughly bilingual, having learned two or more tongues in their childhood. But all this is beside the question.

The basic question is a very simple one: do we or do we not want an international language?

Here we have a most interesting divergence of opinion. Governments, with a few laudable exceptions, do not favor an international language. They are afraid that such a language will loosen their holds upon their respective populations. Despite all the lip service that is paid to the spirit of internationalism, there are few governments that truly favor such a spirit, and the Communist governments are by far the worst offenders in this respect, as evidenced by the infinite stumbling blocks they place in the way of international exchanges of persons, goods and currencies.

People, when they are asked to express their views, invariably react favorably, by majorities that usually hover around the 80 per cent mark. This has been fully demonstrated by Gallup and other polls, taken in all sorts of countries where such polls could be conducted, including our own.[2]

Most interesting is the reaction of professional linguists, the people who ought to be able to supply an expert opinion. From the time when the question began to be seriously discussed, back in the seventeenth century, until the 1920's, language scholars, in their overwhelming majority, favored the creation or adoption of a common language for world intercourse. We need only refer to Jakob von Grimm, who discussed the question at great length;[3] Otto Jespersen, De Saussure, Ogden and Richards, who offered constructed languages of their own; Bréal, Brugmann, Leskien, Courtenay, la Grasserie, Meillet, Meyer, Müller, Leibniz, Kent, Spitzer, Vossler, Schuchardt, Sweet, and many others.[4] It is indeed difficult to find, prior to 1920, any reputable linguist who opposed the general theory of the international language, though many voiced opposition to one specific proposal or another.

This situation has spectacularly changed, at least for what concerns the American picture. Recently a questionnaire on the subject was sent out to 108 professional linguists, most of them Americans. Of the 47 who sent in replies, 18 were in favor of an international language in principle, 27 against, 2 undecided. The writings of the American school of linguistics are replete with forthright rejections not of a particular tongue, but of the general principle.[5]

While the percentages are by no means as decisive as they are in the popular polls, they are such as to give us pause, and call for a careful examination of the reasons alleged for the opposition. (It is hardly necessary to examine the favorable responses; they are based, as are those of laymen, on the tool value of an instrument of international communication; on the possibility of establishing a better international understanding; on the help that such a language will give to trade, travel, scholarship, science; etc.)

The reason most frequently adduced for opposition to the principle of an international language is that language is the expression of a people's culture, and intimately bound up with all other manifestations of this culture. In the view of the opponents, the international language, if selected from among existing natural tongues, would be tantamount to imposing an alien culture, or at least a sizable segment thereof, on the majority of the world's peoples; while if it were to be selected from among the constructed tongues, it would carry no cultural values at all, and therefore never really come alive.

All this is highly reminiscent of the mentalistic position previously described (the intimate link between language and the soul of the people),[6] and it is somewhat surprising that this point of view should stem from members of the American school, which is nothing if not mechanistic and positivistic. In presenting language as a cultural, spiritual activity, they are going over lock, stock and barrel to the enemy's camp.

But perhaps there is something more to their position than a mere logical inconsistency. The American school is closely linked with anthropology, and it is the anthropologists who have been foisting upon us the concept of "culture," not as consisting of the higher manifestations of the human mind and spirit, but as the sum total of a group's activities. Taken in this acceptance, the customs of eating one's enemies, or of burying one's parents alive, which still persist in some remote areas of the earth, are part of a people's "culture."

Without wishing to go into a controversy as to the appropriateness of using the same word in two such contradictory meanings, it may further be remarked that the anthropological linguists are very much in favor of preserving the "cultures" of small and backward groups, in the interests of their own scientific observations and highly specialized research. That in preserving these "cultures" they may be working a disfavor on the groups involved does not seem to worry them.

In the purely linguistic field, given the possibility of keeping a small and backward group speaking its indigenous language, which keeps it from becoming a part of advancing world civilization and culture, or fostering in the midst of that group the study and use of a great world language like English or French, the anthropological linguist would much prefer to continue and encourage the use of the unimportant native dialect.[7] The use of French instead of Creole by the Haitian population would tend to make them a part of a large, important, highly civilized world community, and the use of standard English instead of Pidgin by the natives of Melanesia would in like manner promote their admission to the English-speaking community. Confirming them in their Creole and Pidgin habits may be taking the line of least resistance as far as effort goes, but it also tends to isolate the speakers and confirm them in their backwardness.

An extension of this doctrine would lead national governments to encourage the study and use of local dialects rather than the national tongues, and this at a period when standardized national cultures, and even a standardized world culture, are more and more tending to emerge.

Perhaps all this goes hand in hand with the tendency of anthropological linguists to encourage substandard forms of speech, vulgarisms, localisms and slang, all in the name of "usage." Whatever their purpose may be, the result is clear: to delay material progress, which is built on standardization and unification rather than on diversity.

For what concerns motives, three possibilities present themselves: the first, and most charitable, is that they are inspired by a genuine scientific interest in their subject matter, which is language and languages, coupled with a natural love of the picturesque and varied, and an equally natural reluctance to see the merging and disappearing of the world's folkways into a uniform standard culture which, while it may be more practical and efficient, is necessarily more drab.

The second hypothesis is that they may be subconsciously inspired by a selfish desire to preserve as much as possible of their professional subject matter. Members of the American school of linguistics have been known to voice the direct and ungenerous accusation that those who oppose their points of view and methodologies are inspired by the fear that their income from teaching and textbooks may dwindle if the new methods and new texts conceived by the linguists themselves become the vogue.[8] Have they ever done any soul-searching into their own motives when they oppose the spreading of the world's great languages and the creation or adoption of a single tongue for world use? Could it be that they envisage, in the more or less distant future, a time when their favorite subject matter, the little-known tongues of small, unimportant, semi-civilized or downright savage groups, will have vanished from the scene, as did Iberian and Gaulish before the onset of Latin; and when the substandard, colloquial, slangy and local forms they love so well, and on which they base their mouthings as to the "real" structure of English, will be swallowed up by a standardized general American? What will happen then to their teaching and textbooks?

There is a third possibility, still less flattering, which, by its very nature, can apply to only a few among them, in fully conscious fashion, but which the rest of them follow in the guise of fellow-travelers, without recognizing its implications. This is the desire, implicit in the writings of many members of this school, to weaken the position and prestige of the great languages of Western civilization, and rob them of existing or potential speakers, thus contributing to that *Untergang des Abendlandes* which is so pleasurably anticipated in certain circles, both here and abroad.

The great linguists of the past did not hesitate to put themselves in the forefront of reform movements in language which they deemed beneficial to mankind.[9] Unlike them, the present-day linguistic scientists hold themselves apart and tend to cast ridicule upon such movements.

Spelling reform for a language such as English, and the problem of selecting and putting into operation an international language that will put an end to linguistic incomprehension are two such movements. The average linguistic scientist, overconcerned with registering the delicate shadings of language in the fleeting present, scorns not only the past, but also the future, and often casts covert or open discredit upon those who would channel the future course of language into more rational and less haphazard streams. "Our function is to record, not to direct" seems to be their motto.

The function of an enlightened, free press is also to record, as exactly as possible, the events of the fleeting moment. But no one would call that function complete if the recording of news were not accompanied by reasoned editorial opinion concerning the channeling of future events in the right direction. This is not merely the privilege, but the duty of a press that wishes to describe itself as fully free.

Linguistics should abandon its defeatism, its unwillingness to lead, its supine acceptance of the forces of "usage," and take an active part in language's future, both on the internal and on the international level. What would we think of physicians who limited themselves to describing disease and refused to seek cures? Of lawyers, who described existing laws, good or bad, and made no effort to improve them? Of physicists or chemists, who described the facts of physics or chemistry, and failed to seek beneficial applications?

The linguist should go beyond setting forth the facts of language as he sees them. Language is a human activity, and therefore subject to intelligent guidance and handling, even more than plagues, iron rails and chemical compounds. Language is primarily a human tool for human use. If blind forces have been allowed to shape that tool in the past, there is no reason why they should be allowed to continue to shape it in the future.

Whatever the defeatists and historical determinists among us may think, it is the linguist's task, among others, to shape existing languages so that they may become better, finer, hardier tools for human use, and to try to evolve a form of communication that may eventually lead to world understanding, at first in the purely material sense of the word, later perhaps in that more spiritual, much abused, much misunderstood sense which may ultimately spell out a diminution of conflict, prejudice, hatred, intolerance and war.

NOTES TO PROBLEM XV

1. M. Pei, *One Language for the World*, Devin-Adair, New York, 1958.

2. A Gallup poll of 1952 showed 78 per cent of the people of the United States in favor of an international language to be put into the world's kindergartens and elementary schools on a basis of parity with the national languages, with 15 per cent opposed and 7 per cent undecided. The same question, repeated at the end of 1961, showed 84 per cent in favor, 10 per cent opposed, 6 per cent undecided. A poll taken in Japan in 1960 among foreign tourists to the country, and repeated among Japanese students, showed about 80 per cent of those polled, both Japanese and foreigners, in favor of the idea. In 1952, similar polls taken in Norway, Holland, Finland and Canada showed between 70 and 80 per cent "yes" votes.

3. M. Pei, *One Language for the World,* pp. 104, 151.

4. M. Pei, *op. cit.,* pp. 265 ff.; A Guérard, *A Short History of the International Language Movement,* London, 1922, pp. 211–215.

5. To cite only two examples, see C. Laird, *The Miracle of Language,* World, Cleveland, 1953, p. 284, and R. A. Hall, Jr., *Linguistics and Your Language,* Garden City, 1960, pp. 228–242.

6. See Problem V.

7. See in this connection the UNESCO Report on *The Use of the Vernacular Languages in Education,* Paris, 1953, p. 25, and R. A. Hall, Jr., *Hands Off Pidgin English!* Sydney, 1955.

8. R. A. Hall, Jr., in *French Review,* May 1944, p. 377.

9. Guérard's work, cited above, presents (pp. 211–215, under the heading "Bibliographical Notes") a list of articles on the international language problem by such renowned linguists as Bréal, Brugmann, Courtenay, Jespersen, La Grasserie, Leskien, Meillet, Meyer, Müller, Régnaud, Schuchardt and Sweet.